D0121477

On the Corinthian Spirit

CULT OF GAMES PLAYING MANLINESS 45
VICT. CRICKET PHOTOGS 42-3
CRICKET 67,72ff,
74 M. CLASS SKILLS ADMIN-PROF NIN 73,98
CHECK
EARNINGS CAP 79 (RETAIN SYSTEM?) 107
PRO-AM & WIDER CULT ENV. 83
GENTLEMAN 85,88,101,119 (BOYS'
ROMANTIC SPORTS BIOGRAPHY 116 STORIES)
SPORT AS ROMANTIC ACTIVITY 18
— ABSTRACTED INTERIOR GLORY

On the Corinthian Spirit

BORN NOT MADE 23?
INSINUATION (IN WORDS) 32

The Decline of Amateurism in Sport

110
VIC'NS MADE SPORT RESPECTABLE
— CRICKET HAD CACHET
— GAMBLING 41

D. J. Taylor

+ HYMN, PITCH — CELEB
MATCHES

— GROWTH IN EXPANSE OF 42
HARROW PLAYING FIELDS

— JUSTIFICATION OF ATHLETIC 43
PROWESS IN ITSELF
+ BUT, PERHAPS, A MANLY
STRAIGHTFORWARD 44-5
CHARACTER
— OPPS & PROBS OF MASS AUD 45f.

PROFM IN FOOTBALL LEGAL 1885 49
CORINTHIANS RISE & PEAK 50-2
— MORAL DISTINCTION (VS PROS) 57
— PATRIARCHAL ONE-NATION 59
TORYISM
— VS. PASSIONS & (LOCAL) IDNS 60

ORWELL'S ATTITUDE TO 'GAMES' 61
REP'VE OF HIS TIMES
— MCC
— MORAL 'SSING ON THE ALTAR' 63
— NAT' THINKING 64-5
— IONALISM 65
— CRANK? & THEIR THOUGHTS 66
— AM. CRICKET & ENGLISHNESS 68

Yellow Jersey Press

LONDON
— NOSTALGIA 69

MCC & AMATEUR CODE 98
CELEBS 108
'FAIR PLAY' 109-110

Published by Yellow Jersey Press 2006

2 4 6 8 10 9 7 5 3 1

Copyright © D. J. Taylor 2006

D. J. Taylor has asserted his right under the Copyright, Designs and Patents
Act 1988 to be identified as the author of this work

First published in Great Britain in 2006 by
Yellow Jersey Press

Yellow Jersey Press
Random House, 20 Vauxhall Bridge Road,
London SW1V 2SA

Random House Australia (Pty) Limited
20 Alfred Street, Milsons Point, Sydney,
New South Wales 2061, Australia

Random House New Zealand Limited
18 Poland Road, Glenfield,
Auckland 10, New Zealand

Random House (Pty) Limited
Isle of Houghton, Corner of Boundary Road & Carse O'Gowrie,
Houghton 2198, South Africa

The Random House Group Limited Reg. No. 954009
www.randomhouse.co.uk

A CIP catalogue record for this book is available from the British Library

The publishers and author make grateful acknowledgement to the following
for permission to reproduce lyrics: Warner/Chappell Music Ltd, London W6
8BS for 'Amateur Hour', words & music by Ronald D. Mael © 1974
Warner/Chappell Music Publishing Ltd.

ISBN 9780224075855 (From Jan 07)
ISBN 0 224 075853

Papers used by Random House are natural, recyclable products made from
wood grown in sustainable forests. The manufacturing processes conform to
the environmental regulations of the country of origin

Typeset by SX Composing DTP, Rayleigh, Essex
Printed and bound in Great Britain by
Clays Ltd, St Ives Plc

For John Taylor MBE,
on his eighty-fifth birthday

— NEGLECT OF AMATEUR TRADN
MEANS MISSING OUT ON VITAL
PART OF BEHAVIORAL COCKTAIL
THAT MAKES US WHAT WE ARE
& SHALL BECOME.

Contents

'Serious sport has nothing to do with fair play. It is bound up with hatred, jealousy, boastfulness, disregard of all rules and sadistic pleasure in witnessing violence: in other words it is war minus the shooting.'

George Orwell, 'The Sporting Spirit' (1945)

'All sports are eventually confining.'

Martin Amis

'He spent the morning in a torment of indecision. At lunch, however, his resolution returned to him. As he sat with another fellow smoking a pipe over the coffee, he felt himself filled with an immense courage. He did not tell the other fellow anything of what was in his mind, but talked enthusiastically with him about the prowess of the Corinthians. He pictured the little team of amateurs charging triumphantly through the burly hosts of professionals, while the crowds cheered them to the echo.'

Bryan Guinness, *Singing Out of Tune* (1933)

Acknowledgements

I am grateful to Peter Franzen, editor of the *Eastern Daily Press*, for allowing me to reproduce the greater part of his newspaper's report on the Norwich City versus Corinthians game of January 1929.

Several people suggested promising lines of enquiry or useful reference materials. I should particularly like to thank David Kynaston, Josh Lacey, Paul Willetts and my editor, Tristan Jones.

PROLOGUE

The Umpire Strikes Back

It is a warmish summer Sunday in the late 1980s somewhere in the Oxfordshire countryside and I am sitting on the steps of a rickety cricket pavilion, eyes shaded against the sun, watching the batsmen – ambling white figures, set against an emerald back-cloth – cross and recross. Ten feet away someone's wife or girlfriend is reading a copy of *Orley Farm*. From inside the pavilion male voices bicker and whinny. 'Bob said he was going to give Stephen out for not batting amusingly.' 'What's the point of bringing a blue with us if he gets out for three?' Someone else is asking if anyone happens to be going home in the direction of Ealing. All in all, it is a fairly typical afternoon spent in the company of the Scotts.

In their modest way, the Captain Scott Invitation XI – motto *modo egredior* ('means of egress', i.e., 'I'm just going outside'), complex supporting mythology based on the travails of Sir Robert Falcon Scott – are quite as famous a cricketing proposition as the Lord's

Taverners or I Zingari. At least two books have been written around their exploits. The occasional off-duty celebrity can be found diffidently ornamenting their ranks (Hugh Grant, turning out in the summer of 1993, told a friend of mine that he was acting in some dreadful film about weddings that looked set to be the ruination of his career). They play village sides, college 2nd XIs, obscure aggregations of journalists. The core personnel consists of a gang of minor public school boys who knew each other at Oxford and are now gracing the corridors of accountancy firms in Eastcheap, barristers' chambers in Lincoln's Inn or the labyrinths of Broadcasting House. My own presence here is down less to cricketing ability – career best a haymaking sixteen not out against the Old Talbotians – than a fast friendship with the club secretary. In the course of our opponents' innings, lately concluded, I have featured as a nervous deep mid-off and, in a solitary over of notional off-breaks, conceded thirteen runs. But the Scotts are a kindly and courteous bunch and everybody has been very decent about these failings.

Meanwhile, out on the square the match winds on. Somehow I never remember the progress or statistics of Scott games. Here amid the late summer verdure, atmosphere is all: interminable lunches at the Nag's Head in Oxford, jets of cigarette smoke rising vertically to the sky, the dense hedgerows of cow parsley beyond the boundary. This particular afternoon, though, something is up. Our opponents – the rustics of Charlton-on-Otmoor, say, or New College, are an umpire short and one of our players, a laconic character named Noel Hardy, has agreed to fill the gap. I watch him now as the bowler trundles in, lofts the ball down the pitch in the direction of the Scott batsman – a goodish player called Jim Turner – and hits him on the pad. So far is Turner's bat from the line of the stumps that he doesn't bother to straighten up, leave it in freeze-frame before the umpire's enquiring eye or perform any of the actions that take place on Test Match TV coverage whenever the bowler raises a shout. Unexpectedly, or rather not that unexpectedly, if one knows the Scotts, the standards by which they play and the personal tensions that occasionally seethe beneath these placid surfaces, Noel raises his finger.

What happens? Turner – righteously aggrieved, but uneasily conscious of the club's sporting tradition – glares back, wonders about saying something, thinks better of it, swings his bat savagely under his arm, stalks off the pitch, hurls the bat through the changing room doorway, goes home in a sulk and never plays for the Scotts again. Noel monitors the next few overs with a scrupulousness worthy of Harold 'Dickie' Bird. Later, in the bar of whichever pub to which we have adjourned, he will confess that he took the decision simply 'to stop Jim Turner showing off'. Even here, in the Oxfordshire back lanes with the nightjars swooping in the dusk, it seems a call from a vanished age, like Eton schoolboys of the 1920s watching Queen Mary's coach rattling through the streets of Windsor or the lines of scarlet cavalry drawn up before the heights at Balaclava, a scent at once subtle, elusive and all but vanished from the world – the Corinthian Spirit.

I

1929

But the Corinthian Spirit had wafted over our family history before. My father started watching football in 1929. From the filial vantage point, 1929 is the year of Ramsay MacDonald's second Labour government and the Wall Street Crash, or, to narrow the focus a little, George Orwell's return from washing dishes in Paris to get on with the serious business of becoming a writer, and the crack-up of Evelyn Waugh's first marriage. Eight years old and living in a stuccoed council house on the west side of Norwich, my father knew nothing of these despatches from the wider world. His own universe was bounded by the double row of shops known as Bunnett Square, a quarter-mile to the south, Avenue Road School, three-quarters of a mile to the east in the direction of the city centre, the sanctities of church, hearth and family, and – sometimes seeming to dominate them to the exclusion of all else – the Saturday afternoon activities of Norwich City Football Club.

It was to the Nest, a tiny ground hemmed in by

the surrounding houses and betraying its origins as an ancient chalkpit (to the dismay of fleet-footed wingers, one end concluded in a twenty-foot-high concrete wall) that dad was first taken, on 3 October 1929, to watch Norwich – then a middling indifferent Third Division South side – go down 0-4 to Fulham. My father's only memory of the game, three-quarters of a century later, is of bursting into tears as the second and third goals went in and being consoled by visiting fans with lumps of chocolate.

They shut the Nest on safety grounds in 1935, the year after Norwich won promotion to the Second Division: Carrow Road, its purpose-built replacement, was thrown up in a matter of weeks, between the close of one season and the start of the next. I get the impression, though, that the six years my father spent surveying the Nest's sloping, lopsided patch of turf, only lately reclaimed from its original OS map listing of 'Rump's Hole', were more important to him than the six decades of more upmarket match-day attendance that followed.

His memories of it are a cavalcade of sound, spectacle and personality: the FA Cup fifth round defeat against Sheffield Wednesday when 25,000 people crammed into a space designed for half that number and the crowd spilled on to the pitch; Mr Weekes, the St Leonard's Road barber whose house adjoined the ground and who let out his back bedroom to spectators on match days; the sunlight shining off the demon left-winger Spud Murphy's bald head; the yells of 'Give it to Varco!', the rampaging, thirteen-stone centre-forward who later set up as a fish merchant in his native Cornwall and became Mayor of Fowey.

More interesting even than this, perhaps, is his knack of remembering events that in some cases predate his own presence on the terraces. In particular, he recalls the pained shaking of adult heads that took place at 5 Hodgson Road, Norwich, on the evening of 12 January 1929 shortly after the radio confirmed the startling news that City, having walked over non-league Chatham 6-1 in the first round of the FA Cup and steamrollered Third Division South rivals Newport County 6-0 in the second (Varco 4), had been trounced 0-5 *at home* in the third by an amateur team known as the Corinthians, an entity apparently composed of civil servants, Lloyd's underwriters and ageing public school boys.

By these days, of course, the Corinthians' tornado years were behind them. Nearly a quarter of a century had passed since the last Corinthian held down a berth in the England team. And yet over the ensuing couple of decades an altogether glittering mythology had assembled itself around them. A team whose commitment to the amateur virtues was such that they disdained to take penalties! A team that invariably responded to an injury among the opposition by exiling one of their own players to the touchline to join him! A team that, even now, here in the late 1920s, a player short for most of the game, were capable of giving professional cup opponents a serious run-around.

What testimony remains? To have watched that match and to retain any coherent recollections of it, you would, I calculated, have to be in your late eighties. Norfolk, I assured myself, must be buzzing with such characters, hale octogenarians with total recall memories, who, teacup in one hand to represent the ball, sugar lumps in the other to represent the retreating defence, would obligingly re-enact one of Varco's fruitless assaults on goal. Confident of turning up some reminiscent scene-sweller from the dawn of footballing time, I advertised in the local paper. I got two replies: one from a man who had written, and self-published, a rather good paperback on the pre-history of Arsenal FC; the other from an eighty-nine-year-old named Mr Tom Boys, present at the game, who remembered . . . almost exactly nothing, except for an enraged Norwich fan yelling at the referee, Mr Chamberlain, 'Come you hare, I'll muster you!', a slang expression so recondite as not even to appear in Professor Peter Trudgill's *The Norfolk Dialect*.

No luck with oral history, then. It was time to turn to official sources. Delving into the Eastern Counties Newspapers archive not long afterwards, I turned up the account of the game that appeared thirty-six hours later in the local morning paper, the *Eastern Daily Press*. Twenty thousand people, it emerged, had turned out to witness this humiliation, five thousand more than the previous record attendance against Bath in 1923. Gate receipts were a lavish £1591. Further period garnishes can be observed in the presence of the Lord Mayor and Sheriff, a brass band and the sight of the spectators 'standing bare-headed and singing the National Anthem – an impressive spectacle'. As for the game itself, the *EDP*'s discreetly impartial reporter registered 'a smashing blow to Norwich City's prestige'. The merit of the Corinthians' performance was enhanced 'by the fact that the amateurs not only overcame the generally acknowledged disadvantages of playing on a strange and closely confined ground, but after the first ten minutes they were reduced in number through an injury to R. G. Jenkins and practically gained their victory with ten men'. Victory in these circumstances, our man in the stand with the Trilby hat and the bar of Caley's Marching Chocolate averred, 'is at all times noteworthy, but the wide margin of the Corinthians' success made it a surprising and almost remarkable achievement'.

What, from the Norwich point of view, went wrong? A canter through the column-long match report discloses the usual catalogue of home-team mistakes. 'The second goal was virtually a gift', chided our reporter. 'The mere fact of an appeal having been made does not excuse players from taking it for granted that official ruling will be in agreement with their views. Playing to the whistle is still sound advice.' In the end, though, it all came down to technique. 'The better method, the superior skill, was unquestionably on the side of the Corinthians. In many respects the display of the amateurs was a fine object lesson.' With a front line led by the dashing centre-forward Claude Ashton, who scored a hat-trick, the Corinthians got by on speed and penetration. Ashton, according to his Monday morning appraiser, 'whether at half-back or forward . . . has never been anything else than a great player and worthy of being ranked with the famous Corinthians of a previous generation. The fact that he scored three goals emphasises the value of his good shooting to the side, and he was clever enough to keep his wing going single-handed.'

Subsequently, the Corinthian full-back, A. G. Bower, provided a 'Captain's Comment' of quite startling modesty. There was little between the two sides, he declared, 'except that we finished off in front of goal a little better'. The Norwich side 'struck me as being too individual in their play. There was not enough cohesion.' He concluded by commending the atmosphere in which the match had been played. 'It was a hard game, and the Norwich players were good, clean, sporting men who congratulated us on our victory and wished us every luck in the Cup.'

What happened next? As the *Eastern Daily Press* sapiently observed, 'How far the Corinthians will be able to carry the amateurs' banner through the present competition will depend a great deal on the luck of the draw and the game.' In *How Steeple Sinderby Wanderers Won the FA Cup*, J. L. Carr's great comic novel of serial giant-killing, the village side of Sinderby is drawn away to mighty Leeds. Here 'young Billy Sledmer, tearing at greyhound pace into the empty Leeds half' scores the winning goal with ten minutes to spare. A. G. Bower and his bank clerks were denied their chance of glory. In the fourth round the Corinthians were drawn away to First Division West Ham and went down 3-0. 1929, it turns out, was the Corinthians' swansong. In 1930 they lost a twice-replayed third-round tie to Second Division Millwall. A year later they suffered a 2-1 defeat at Second Division Port Vale. Between 1934 and 1939 they registered only three goals in five FA Cup appearances. Come 1939 they opted to amalgamate with another like-minded amateur outfit to form the Corinthian Casuals. Then came six years of war, which blew the last vestiges of the amateur tradition in top-grade English football to shreds. The days of Claude Ashton, A. G. Doggart and K. E. Hegan, and before that a roster of unpaid talent extending deep into the 1880s, were gone.

My father, on the other hand, pursued a decent amateur career with the 1st XI of the Norwich Union Insurance Company, whose headquarters he joined as a clerk in 1937, won a Norwich Business Houses Championship medal in 1947 and, on the strength of this endorsement, later applied for the vacant manager's job at Exeter City. He never got a reply.

II

Strickland of the Sixth

For a brief period of my life, three and a half decades ago, I was a sporting hero myself.

The evidence came to light the other day, wedged into a long-unopened cardboard box in the attic between a stack of twenty-five-year-old Christmas cards and some book reviews that I may have contributed to the *Independent* at about the time of the Hillsborough disaster in 1989: ivory-tinted press cuttings sheared from the *Norfolk Mercury* and the *Pink 'Un*, the Norwich Saturday evening sports sheet; match statistics typed up on my father's frail, pre-war Remington on the back of paper stamped with the logo of something called the Institute of Supervisory Management. The 14th Norwich Cubs XI, whose left wing I ornamented, had a good season in 1970–71. I discover that, playing in the Bobby Charlton division of the local Cub league, we won sixteen out of our seventeen fixtures, took thirty-two out of a maximum thirty-four points and scored 152 goals to our opponents' 13. (Cub football tended to magnify the usual differences of age, physique and ability: a moderate team of burly ten-year-olds playing a mediocre bunch of nine-year-olds would expect to win 10-0 or 15-0.) Of those 152 goals, 42 came courtesy of my searing left foot.

Looking back at the stats, which my father would log meticulously each Sunday morning at the dining-room table, I am rather impressed by how good I was, or appear to have been. Other habitués of the 14th Norwich forward line – B. Downes, say, P. Sheridan or P. Crocker – might collect the odd brace or register the occasional hat-trick, but the real spadework, the decisive shift in that 139-digit goal difference, was accomplished by D. Taylor here. Four in the 8-2 demolition of the 13th Norwich in February 1971, five in the 20-1 steamrollering of Brooke a fortnight later, six, even, in a pitiless 15-0 late-season evisceration of the 36th Norwich. And not content with knocking in fistfuls against lower-table makeweights, our man had a beady eye for the big occasion. Proof? The famous grudge match of 13.3.71 against the 27th Norwich, when, after a tense forty minutes of stalemate, the ball squirted out of a goal-mouth melee, bobbed off my out-stretched right shin and described an outsize parabola whose descending arc took it a few inches below the 27th's crossbar and above the grasp of their mute, imploring goalkeeper.

Curiously enough, I have hardly any individual memories of that balmy six months or so of pre-teen sporting glory. A few black and white photos disgorged from an old album showing the team lining up for the inter-divisional final (we lost 1-2 to the 26th Norwich) reassured me that I could still identify the other boys. Billy Downes is the flaxen-haired kid with the goofy smile. Terry Brookes, the only one among us who could really play, broods seriously over the match ball. D. Taylor – tall, pudgy, with Bugs Bunny teeth – stands resolutely by. The events on the pitch, though, those charged configurations of fresh-faced ten-year-olds ('Stephen', I can remember someone warning our gutsy right-half S. Davies, 'if you keep tackling like that you'll break someone's leg'), nearly always escape me. All that remains, in fact, is a kind of collective memory, of something that may not ever have happened precisely as I recollect but came close enough to it, and on so many occasions, to give the sequence of events a kind of archetypal rosy sheen.

It is a Saturday afternoon, let us say, in February 1971 and I am ten years old, standing on a three-quarter-size football pitch in the grounds of Blackdale School on the outskirts of south-west Norwich. Grey mist, newly risen from the Cringleford marshes and the water meadows of the University of East Anglia, hangs low over the field, partly obscuring the twenty or thirty spectators (among them my father, the cub pack's chain-smoking Akela, Mrs Barron, and two Dickensian characters named Mr Moss and Mr Downes who purport to manage the side) and causing the shouts and cries from fifty yards away to echo from a netherworld of dimly glimpsed figures and shadowy half-light. Even in the hairy knee-length shorts that my mother makes me wear in preference to the flimsy loincloths doled out to the other boys, it is glacially cold – that famous East Anglian chill born of a wind blown down from Jutland with nothing to stand in its way bar icy sea. None of these absurdities, of course, matters in the least. Already, such is my passion for football, I have played in thunderstorms, in continuous, pitch-liquefying downpours, on rolled snow with touchlines and penalty spots picked out by indefatigable pre-teen hands. What matters – the subject of endless romantic daydreamings, mental replayings and rapt, interior rehearsals – is the pattern of the next thirty seconds.

What happens? Abruptly the ball rolls out from some midfield scrimmage to the remote, unmarked position I occupy on the extreme left-hand touchline; gratefully I collect it on my toe. A half-back emerges tentatively out of the murk but I dab the ball carefully to one side of him and then tear over his haplessly committed leg away down the left wing. I'm a big lad for ten (sadly the onset of puberty will reduce me to average height and weight), and prospective school 100-metres champion, and I get the feeling that most of the opponents I come up against here on the Elysian fields of childhood don't especially want to tangle with me. The full-back, a timorous looking nine-year-old, divines something of this superiority as he approaches and shies away with only the briefest attempt to engage. Somewhere in the region of the penalty spot B. Downes, P. Sheridan and P. Crocker are clamouring for the pass, but this is cub football, where the ego invariably wins out and I scamper unheedingly on. Just the goalkeeper to beat, then.

To the right of the goalposts, hands plunged into his overcoat pocket, centre-parted Brylcreemed hair unruffled by the wind, stands my father, murmuring that exemplary piece of coach's wisdom 'Far post!', but the situation is too far gone for procedural niceties, those textbook jinks and strokes and subtleties. Finding the ball still providentially stuck to my left foot – there have been times when, in my anxiety to score, I've hared off down the wing with the vital accessory becalmed in a divot – I simply blast it straight at the keeper, a lymphatic ten-year-old who sinks brokenly to his knees as the net – if there is a net – billows behind him. The last things I see are my father's hands raised above his head in exaltation.

Soccer – sport generally – is essentially a romantic activity. For all the variety of disguises in which the game habitually presents itself, there is no getting away from this. The act of pulling on a pair of football boots may double up as a search for companionship, or better health, or half a dozen other localised amenities, but it is also the pursuit of a certain kind of abstracted interior glory – the 'personal myth' of Anthony Powell's *A Dance to the Music of Time*, in which what happens to you is in the end much less important than what you think happens to you or, perhaps more vitally, what other people think. Sport's romantic gloss – the epic victory snatched out of the jaws of defeat, the ten-man fight back against overwhelming odds, the plucky minnow seeing off the vainglorious whale – is also what makes it so difficult to write about, above the level of the back-page match report. Somehow anatomising soccer in the grandiloquently empurpled prose of the top-of-the-range cricket book (the Cardus–Arlott type, in which boundaries are invariably 'sweetly struck', or, if the chap really fancies himself, 'smote') seems horribly inappropriate, if only because of the blatant distance between the medium and the physical reality of the thing described. A useful comparison, perhaps, is with fictional accounts of sex – again, conceived of by the average novelist as a romantic activity, yet hedged about (if one treats it 'realistically') with unromantic physical detail. To put it another way, in trying to re-imagine what adult consciousness conceives as youthful forays across the greensward one tends to forget about the sore knees, the smell of embrocation and the wet blanket of a provincial Sunday hanging across the horizon.

But where precisely, in those dense yet fleeting afternoons at Blackdale School, with Messrs Moss and Downes bellowing from the touchline and the clouds drifting in across the pale Norfolk sky, did the romance lie? Part of it was to do with sheer sensation: the acres of green grass, the goal looming towards you, the rictus of agony on the goalkeeper's face. A bit more, perhaps, was to do with the tremendous detonation of confidence that sporting prowess brings to an academically minded ten-year-old boy. Top marks in French meant a compass point jabbed in your leg. The prestige of a hat-trick, on the other hand, was ungainsayable. There was also – and even as a child I think I appreciated a little of this – the scent of a social divide momentarily transcended, in that I lived in a four-bedroom house in a middle-class suburb and went to prep school while the rest of the team mostly dwelt in council houses on the teeming Earlham estate. And yet, far more important than these peripheral advantages was the seductive mythological landscape opened up by the sight of *D. Taylor (6)* on a piece of foolscap paper. Ultimately, those forty-two goals, that succession of agonised defenders and billowing nets, was the closest I ever came to being Strickland of Havenhall School.

'Strick' (forename unknown) was the hero of R. A. H. Goodyear's novel *Strickland of the Sixth* (1928). There were other examples of Goodyear's compendious *oeuvre* in the shelf of boys' school stories bestowed on me by my father – *The White House Boys*, say, or *The Fellows of Ten Trees School* – and other heroes, but Strickland was the one who appealed most to my imagination. Fresh-faced, square-jawed, barrel-chested and presumably in sight of his eighteenth birthday, Strick was the captain of Havenhall, a public school (somewhere in North Yorkshire to judge from the townee accent) sunk into decay by dint of its inaccessibility. Entry in the local football charity cup, carried through in the face of seething internal opposition, seems a fail-safe way of upping the establishment's profile. Apart from a couple of subplots (in which a crooked lawyer hoodwinks several schoolboys into buying valueless plots of land in a local field, and White Hart, an abandoned Red Indian boy from the local circus, is adopted by the school porter), *Strickland of the Sixth*'s 250 or so large-print pages are about football. In the first round the Havens take on Asheltubla, a backstreet apprentice boys' side, and win 1-0, narrowly avoiding a riot provoked by their opponents' vengeful fans ('This referee's bin agin us all through. Pay him out boys.'). A head-magisterial ban on subsequent participation is rescinded at the last minute, allowing Strick's men comfortably to defeat Thameswold Junior Swifts in round two. There follows a tense semi-final standoff against the local bank clerks team, won by a single goal in the dying moments. One down in the final against the brawny mechanicals of Gissen's Motor Works, the Havens stage an astonishing fight back to emerge victorious by the odd goal in three. In the meantime, the water shortage has been solved by White Hart's powers of divination, while twinkly-eyed old Mr Gissen promises the school a fleet of motor buses.

To the summit of each of these sporting inclines marches the towering figure of 'Strick': cool, resourceful, tight-lipped and a walking embodiment of the manly virtues. Faced with the pitch-side may-hem and the threatened referee of the Asheltubla fixture, he simply squares up to the leading inter-loper and knocks him out cold. Confronted with a quartet of backsliding team-mates, keen to shirk a practice game for an afternoon's blackberrying, he offers to take them all on ('A pulsing pause followed. Each man avoided the captain's level gaze – he was not one whom it was easy to stare down. His searching eyes seemed almost to lay bare what a fellow was actually thinking.'); cravenly the delinquents hasten off to the training ground. Having scored the winner against the bank clerks, our 'blue-eyed and aristocratic young captain' badly injures himself in the final while netting a precious equaliser but refuses to leave the field ('You'll have to go off, old man, I'm afraid', a team-mate sympathises. 'Shall I? Not likely! . . . Not while I can stand on one leg, anyhow. We're a winning side, old lad, if we put on full steam.'). At a final-chapter tea party, the headmaster announces that, having been at the school twenty-one years, 'I can declare with conviction that Havenhall never had a leader like Strick' – here the head lays an affectionate hand on the blushing captain's sleeve – 'and it's quite impossible ever to have a better.'

What did I admire about Strickland? Physical courage and ability, obviously – that eternal swot's veneration of the boy who, mysteriously, knows when to play forward rather than to play back, while cultivating a steely, man-of-few-words laconicism in the face of tricky situations ('I'll shove the wheel into the ribs of the next man who tries that game on' etc). But above all the scent of an effortless superiority, the thought that Strick and his chums were good at games because of an innate, God-given ability, so innate that they barely needed to practise.

There is a rather revealing moment in the match against Thameswold Junior Swifts when some of the junior Havens begin to fraternise with the opposing supporters. The local lads are friendly, but anxious to find reasons for the public school boys' greater skill. 'You've got what we haven't – a man to train you', one of them suggests. No, the Havens assure him: in fact their sports master 'has no truck with footer at all'. Well then, another youngster rationalises, it must be because the Havenhall team gets more practice. No again, he is briskly informed. 'Our captain's had all on to get them to practise once a week even.' 'But look how well they play together . . .'

As a privately educated ten-year-old whose father had escaped some years earlier from the thraldom of the council estate, I rather liked this explanation and the moral universe that seemed to give it sanction. Fair play, hard knocks and sportsmanship – all the virtuous expressions of the amateur spirit, given greater resonance by the assumption that the true sportsman is born not made.

Good old Strick! He lasted three or four years in my imagination, until Gordon Comstock, the midget, paranoiac anti-hero of Orwell's *Keep the*

Aspidistra Flying, with his rants at the literary editors who wouldn't publish his poems and his take-it-or leave-it attitude to women (who, mysteriously, still found him attractive), came and blew him away.

It is 1971 and I am ten years old. Mr Heath is in Downing Street, or sailing his yacht, *Morning Cloud*, along the Solent. Mr Wilson (whom both my parents roundly deplore) is sucking up to the TUC somewhere. The Beatles have split. The Queen is at Buckingham Palace, or taking her ease forty miles down the road from us at Sandringham. The 14th Norwich Cubs are champions of the Bobby Charlton division and, at a fish and chip supper hosted by our Akela, I receive a small gilt-cum-plastic championship medal wrapped up in tissue paper and placed in a tiny cardboard box. What happens next? Most of the team turn eleven and are superannuated into the Scouts, where there isn't a football league. I move up to the third form of Norwich School, which plays rugby in the winter and hockey in the spring, and effectively retire from the game.

Sometimes, wandering around the Earlham estate where I used to deliver papers, past the gates of the branch library or the old cub hut on Colman Road, I wonder what happened to them all: to B. Downes and P. Sheridan and A. Wilkinson, the goalkeeper, and stalwart Terry Brookes. Occasionally in the intervening years, the decades spent in Oxford and London, far away from the Great Eastern Land, those queer, sequestered horizons made up of church towers, brooding heaths and slanting train tracks, news would filter back. Silk Cut-smoking Mrs Barron (whose phone number I find I can remember after thirty-five years) is dead. Philip Crocker married the mother of one of my eldest son's school friends. Someone else's name turned up in a local-paper scandal involving assaults and common-law wives. Stephen Davies, whose parents ran the grocer's shop on Bunnett Square, joined the army. All you would expect, in fact, from a bunch of lads from the west Norwich estates and lower-bourgeois thoroughfares brought together by a shared interest in the beautiful game. As for Strickland of the Sixth – that seventy-year-old fig-ment of a retired public school master's imagination – he died on the Normandy beaches, out in the North African desert or along the Burma railway. His legacy, on the other hand, burns defiantly on.

III

Marlon

The great thing about parenthood, thirteen years'
experience of that state insists, is continuity. Just as
my father gave up a fair proportion of his Saturday
afternoons to pace the touchline at Blackdale
School, so, three and a half decades later, I give up a
fair proportion of my Saturday mornings to stalk the
perimeters of the UEA Sports Park – a stone's
throw, it turns out, from the spot where D. Taylor,
B. Downes and P. Sheridan terrorised opposition
defences back in the year of decimal coinage and
'Coz I Luv You'. The object in view is not the 14th
Norwich Cubs but a seven-a-side outfit called the
Eaton Eagles, of which, rather like Mr Moss and Mr
Downes thirty-five years ago, I am the notional
manager.

Management of the Eagles, who play in the
Norfolk Christian Youth League Under-14 division,
and whose ranks include my elder sons, Felix and
Benjy, consists of turning up at the Wednesday
night training sessions, harassing non-paying

parents for their subs, fixing transport to the god-
forsaken villages out on the Norfolk flat where away
games take place and enjoying knowledgeable
touchline conversations with Andy, the coach ('Shall
we give Edward ten minutes now?' 'Might as well.
After all, his dad's come.'). Not much has changed,
and what has is a matter of incidentals. My father
used to watch the 14th in a herringbone overcoat, a
collar and tie and a pair of wash-leather gloves. I
turn up in jacket, jeans and Doc Martens. The kids
fit all the well-established behavioural and physical
patterns I remember from my own childhood. The
shy ones. The rowdy ones. The wiry, athletic con-
tenders. The plump, lolloping no-hopers. It takes all
sorts. The old social contradistinctions still apply,
which is to say that the boys from the breadline
council houses invariably have the flashest trainers.
They are good boys, tolerant boys, *sporting* boys.
This is the Norfolk Christian Youth League, after
all, and the atmosphere on the touchline seems a
good deal less volcanic than it was back in the days
of the Bobby Charlton division, when at least one
match came close to ending in a punch-up.

Still, something here has altered. It is not just that
the kids call me 'David' whereas I called Mr Moss
'Mr Moss', or that divorce and separation have
exponentially bulked out the list of addresses and
contact telephone numbers (*no one* was divorced

when I was ten: I didn't know a single child without two parents resident in the same house.) What has changed – a tiny, abstract detail, maybe in the administration of a boys' football team, its tense alliances, its vague tactics, its tearful languor – is the presence of boys like Marlon. Marlon? In fact, Marlon doesn't play for us but for a rival team from South Park Avenue. Twelve years old. Comes from the Northfields estate. Hair a dusting of charcoal bristles. Thirty-five years ago I knew lots of kids like Marlon, whose dads worked in the boot and shoe factories and whose mums joined the pram promenades at Bunnett Square around the time the local evening paper came on sale, whose family budgets sometimes didn't run as far as summer holidays or even telephones: streetwise, sharp, genetically primed to give middle-class boys such as myself the runaround but restraining themselves out of sheer good nature.

In later life, no question, Marlon will fetch up as a nightclub bouncer, the real-life equivalent of, say, Big Mal in Martin Amis's 'State of England' ('Good evening to you, gentlemen. No I'm sorry, gentlemen. Gentlemen, this club is members only. Oi! Look, hold up, lads. Gentlemen!') zealously guarding the portals of some thronged stoat-hatch in the Prince of Wales Road. For the moment, though, Marlon is merely the most technically accomplished player that the Eagles come up against. Marlon! Half a dozen times a half I find my gaze straying to the right midfield position that Marlon has made so diligently his own. Unlike most of the boys, Marlon has clearly put in an hour or two of study, done a bit of homework, sat silent in front of *Match of the Day* or watched the live games on Sky. He has the TV tricks, the jinks, the dinks, the heft. An overhit pass rolling away in the direction of the corner flag? Marlon will be there monitoring its progress, arms outstretched, legs backpedalling, defying his opponent's intruding toe. Everyone does it, Wayne, Rio and all the molten gods of the small screen.

The other week I watched, fascinated, as Marlon slid in dextrously to tackle a boy even chunkier than he was. It was an exemplary performance – the big kid upended on the all-weather surface, the ball coaxed deviously out into the light – emphatically *not* a foul ('Play the ball, not the man') and yet . . . I looked at Andy the coach. Andy looked at me. Shortly afterwards I glanced over at Marlon again, trying to find an adjective for the look on his face as, silent and serious, he contemplated the fallen body of his opponent. A *resolute* look? No. An *efficient* look. No, again. The word I was searching for, I eventually decided, was *professional*.

IV

Word-Hoard

'Amateur hour goes on and on,
and when you turn pro
You know, she'll let you know . . .'
Sparks, 'Amateur Hour' (1974)

One of the fascinations of language is its capacity for change. This tends to happen without warning, often in unexpected directions, usually to the great discomfort of the persons whose quasi-official responsibility it is to monitor language from on high. However unappealing some of its manifestations there is something faintly reassuring about the process that throws up a word like 'chav' or 'pramface', the thought of ordinary life suddenly shouldering its way on to a photograph previously airbrushed into conformity by newspapers and television. We inhabit a world in which, routine noises about 'freedom of speech' notwithstanding, the formal expression of what one thinks is actually pretty tightly controlled. In these circumstances, the discovery that language has a life of its own, is always one jump ahead of the custodians of the word-hoard, can be a bracing experience, if not without its incidental confusions. Browsing in early Victorian novels, for example, I used regularly to scratch my head at the spectacle of a character, who plainly didn't rate the attractions of the person he was talking about, declaring, 'I don't half like him' in apparent ignorance of the irony that currently attends the usage. Lexicographical enquiry revealed that at some point in the early Victorian period, and for reasons now beyond recall, the phrase's original meaning of 'on a scale of one to ten I like him less than five' began to mutate into its polar opposite.

The same kind of incremental re-invention affects the relationship between the words 'amateur' and 'professional', both of which at the close of the nineteenth century meant practically the reverse of their current definitions. 'Amateur' was defined as someone who did what he did for the sheer love of doing it; the modern notion of 'cack-handed novice' lay far across the horizon. The word 'professional', on the other hand, barely existed as a noun. There were 'professions', of course – destiny-conscious small boys at their prep schools would count out cherry stones to a recitation of 'Army, Church, law, medicine . . .' – but a *professional* meant someone who did something (usually, but not exclusively,

sporting) for money. Both words came weighed
down with a solid freight of insinuation. The title
that E. W. Hornung attached to the adventures of
his gentleman-burglar hero Raffles was *The Amateur
Cracksman*. At the time of publication – 1899 – this
worked as a kind of mitigating gloss, the implication
being that the qualities of genteel sportsmanship
that Raffles brought to his cricketing exploits would
somehow be reproduced in his career as a safe-
breaker.

But who, a century later, would care to be
described as an 'amateur'? If there is one state to
which the average twenty-first-century worker
aspires it is the glossy, cast-iron prestige of the
'professional', with its imputations of expertise,
competence and status. One of my most vivid
memories of working in the City is of the racked
denizens of the Coopers & Lybrand marketing
department consoling themselves with the thought
that, as one of the assistant managers used to put it,
'We are all professionals'. *No we aren't*, I always
wanted to yell out in the course of these therapeutic
conferrings. According to the tradition in which I
was raised, professionals demonstrate their professionalism by passing exams and acquiring letters
after their name, not by spending three years
straightening the pencils in an advertising agency, or
– in my own case – sitting in a basement off Oxford

Street pretending to edit *Airfix Magazine*.

Needless to say, this kind of transformation can be observed several rungs further along the cultural ladder. Here, for example, are the results of an hour or so's pursuit of *amateur* and *professional* through the upper reaches of late twentieth-century English literature. Modish Dr Faber in A. S. Byatt's *Still Life* (1985), a 1950s-era Cambridge academic listening to the pleas of an aspiring Ph.D. student, is prepared to pay amateurism a backhanded compliment. Only nine doctorates have been awarded in English since the war, he tells Frederica Potter. 'The English respect for amateur muddling through is a major reason for the few successes there have been.' In Simon Raven's *Close of Play* (1962), on the other hand, you suspect that the author – no great lover of professionalism in his voluminous cricket writings – is merely being tongue in cheek. At one point a confiding young couple named Ronnie and Mavis conduct an 'earnest professional conversation' in the back seat of a car: in fact the pair are about to perform a sex act before a drawing room full of jaded aristocratic patrons. A bit later, Hugo Warren, Raven's louchely amoral anti-hero, is busy seducing his business associate's wife while trying to persuade her to help him swindle her absent husband. 'We can't go changing arrangements', he lectures the moistly complaisant Nancy. 'It's unprofessional'.

Lest this should sound unexpectedly dutiful, it may be remarked that the 'profession' hereby advertised is a combination of high-class pimping and running chemmy tables.

Here in the 1960s 'profession' does at least have some faint commercial tang. By the time of Anthony Powell's *Journals* (1995–7) 'professional' simply means 'what one is known for or adept at'. Thus one acquaintance of Powell's finds himself marked down as 'a professional seducer', another as a 'professional bad-tempered man', in the same way that a chronic social irritant might be described as a 'professional bore'. Then there is the increasingly common usage of the merely expedient: a 'professional attitude' is one that doesn't falter from the task in hand, plays it by the book, judges the game (metaphorical or otherwise) by the results. Covering the spite-strewn Republican Convention of 1988, Martin Amis got talking to some well-briefed representatives of the 'pollster and media consultant community'. It was a curious, if not chastening, experience. 'Here', he reported back, 'all values are expedient and professionalized, and politics – fascinatingly – is discussed in strictly apolitical terms.'

Still, throughout all these myriad constructions there runs the thought of an expertise whose status is somehow licensed, exam-sanctioned or at least peer-authenticated. In the rows that habitually attend each autumn's award of the Man Booker Prize for Fiction there generally comes a moment when some grand literary panjandrum pronounces that the prize should acquire 'professional judges'. And what exactly is a 'professional judge'? The Merton Professor of English Literature at the University of Oxford? The Literary Editor of the *Sunday Times*? Me? In an average year I might review seventy books in half a dozen different newspapers and magazines, but that doesn't make me a professional literary critic, not according to my scale of values, which insists that to count as a 'professional' at something you should have at least studied it at university. My father, discussing the upper-echelon jobs available at his place of work, would practically bow his head at the mention of the word 'actuary'. Actuaries had to pass exams. The letters FIA after your name meant something in a way that his own professional suffix MISM – obtained, so far as I gathered, by paying an annual subscription – did not. Perhaps, in the end, 'professional' simply means serious, committed, *undeviating*. Here, for example, is the veteran Los Angeles porn star Randy Spears discussing his calling with the *Observer*'s Andrew Anthony:

> But later on he told me that one of the attractions of the job was that he got to have sex with new young

girls. 'I'm still a red-blooded American,' he said. He estimated that there was a 'connection' with a female performer in about three out of ten scenes. Given the conditions in which the scenes take place – with fifteen men looking on, cameras and booms poking from every angle, and the stop–start rhythm of film-making – this seemed to be an astonishing rate of success. In the other seven scenes, said Spears, 'You're just being a professional'.

Professor John Carey, late incumbent of the Merton Chair, Sir Horace Foodle QC with his rheumy eye bent upon the Woolsack, game Randy carving his notches on the LA duplex bedposts, and the man who comes to mend the boiler – they are all *professionals*, you see, all hedged about with licence and protocol and prestige, and the jargon that envelopes their activities is a kind of spiritual body armour. To a Premiership soccer manager the chatter about 'quality', 'zonal marking' and 'Christmas tree' formations is what *langue et parole* is to a semiotician: a figurative caste-mark demanding that what he does for a living be taken seriously.

And where does all this leave the amateur, formerly the symbol of fair play and a stout heart, now become the watchword for terminal second-rateness and lower-rung incompetence? Curiously enough, the moment at which the dwindling status of that word in the public imagination was first brought home to me back in the late 1970s, not on a sports field or in some august commercial chamber, but on a school debating platform. It was the opening round of the *Observer*–Mace competition and Norwich School had been drawn against the Norwich High School for Girls. The motion before us, to be proposed by yours truly and a boy named Matthew Andrews, was 'This house regrets the decline of the amateur'.

Debates between boys' schools and girls' schools in the late 1970s followed an unshiftable pattern. The motion ('This house believes Women's Lib has gone too far', 'This house has no confidence in the United Nations', etc) having been put before the assembled throng, most of whom were more interested in the chat-up possibilities offered by the post-debate coffee and biscuits, a teenage boy – noteless and insouciant – would rise to propose. Ignoring the subject's moral or philosophical aspects, he would discourse, more or less wittily, on whichever peripheral topics caught his eye to gales of respectful male laughter. The participating girls, meanwhile, would sit there stony-faced. *What was all this about?* you could see them thinking. The *Times* articles they had consulted on the subject in the school library the other day hadn't had anything to say about *that*. Finally, when the gales of respectful laughter had died away, the lead girl would jump to her feet, sheaf of notes clutched tightly to her chest and, detonations of remorseless, laugh-free logic exploding in her wake, proceed to blow the motion into fragments.

Allowing for a few minor detours, this was what happened on that far-off night at the Norwich High School for Girls. Opening the debate, I invoked the spirit of Strickland. I pictured my opponents, advantageously clad and gracefully disposed, on the tennis court, the epitome of the amateur spirit. Love over gold, I breezily deposed. I didn't just regret the decline of the amateur, ladies and gentlemen, I rhapsodically concluded, I *mourned* him.

All this went down a storm. Then the first High School speaker, an immensely brainy and beautiful girl named Diana Sutton-Jones, got to her feet. *Flattened* I thought, watching the dense sheaf of notes being drawn tighter to Miss Sutton-Jones's green school-blazered frontage. *Can't live in this league. No shape, no form.* 'Ladies and gentlemen,' Miss Sutton-Jones began, in those precise, no-nonsense tones that sent fourth formers scurrying into the sports pavilion like frightened fowl, 'if you'd fallen down in the street with a heart attack and a man came rushing through the crowd shouting "Let me through, I'm an amateur doctor" you wouldn't be very pleased . . .' You could see the audience beginning to settle itself. No surprises here, then. Watch that girl go! Once again relentless logic was about to blow away fancy-dan dilettante whimsy.

And so it turned out. This house did not regret the decline of the amateur. He couldn't live in this league. No shape, no form. He hadn't the professional qualifications, the A levels, the City and Guilds, the St John Ambulance Brigade certificate. Any attempt to defend him sounded, well, amateurish. What had seen him off, I divined, as Miss Sutton-Jones stuffed her notes back into the depths of her reticule, accepted the adjudicator's congratulations and declined my offer of a post-debate coffee, was the professional touch.

V

Annals of the Corinthians

A century before it had all been very different.

Like much else in nineteenth-century English culture, it took the Victorians to make sport respectable. Cricket, with its top-hatted slip-catchers and ducal sponsors had always had a certain cachet, and the upper end of the hunting field remained firmly aristocratic; but beneath these exalted redoubts came a sprawling, near-medieval chaos of apprentice boys kicking inflated pigs' bladders and village free-for-alls. Sport, to an early Victorian writer like Thackeray, meant cock-fighting, rat-catching and bare-knuckle boxing – all the enticing and semi-legal pastimes documented in Pierce Egan's *Life in London; or The Day and Night Scenes of Jerry Hawthorn Esq. and Corinthian Tom* (1821), the pre-Reform Bill-era man about town's sporting bible. *Vanity Fair*'s sporting similes – the occasion, for example, on which Jos Sedley, drunk beyond redemption at Vauxhall Gardens, hits out 'like Molineaux' – are mostly drawn from prize-fighting.

This faintly disreputable air was enhanced by a long-standing association with gambling. Vast areas of working-class recreation – rowing, for example, or the north of England athletics circuit – were kept alive by betting. Even at the celebrity cricket matches that were a feature of the age (Alfred Mynn, Fuller Pitch and the legendary Felix, say, turning out against the gentlemen of Surrey) a transit camp of bookmakers' tents could be found drawn up alongside the fashionable carriages on the boundary.

If 'games' entered the Victorian age both improvised and unregulated, they left it codified, tightly controlled and, even at their lower reaches, comparatively genteel. The impetus behind this gradual process of sanitisation came, inevitably, from the public schools and the universities. The Oxford versus Cambridge cricket match had been inaugurated as early as 1827; the Boat Race two years later. Thackeray went to what sounds like the inaugural staging in 1829 and reported, 'It is rather a fine sight that boat race particularly on a day when Nature conspireth with ale to render the race pleasant to the see-ers thereof.' Come the mid-century new varieties of sporting encounter followed at the rate of two or three a decade: a tennis fixture in 1859, an athletics tournament in 1864, a rugby match in 1872, a soccer equivalent two years later. If no other yardstick remained, some idea of the enthusiasm which the public schools brought to their recreations – a branch of school life that had formerly been entirely unofficial – could be gauged from the sheer volume of land bought or leased on which to practise them. Between 1845 and 1900, for example, the extent of the Harrow playing fields increased from eight acres to 146. At Marlborough, over the same period, the figure rose from two to sixty-eight.

Activity of this kind required a serious financial commitment from the growing band of mid-Victorian meadow-drainers and land-leasers who laboured at its core. The sum collected at Harrow for use on athletics facilities in the Victorian period was put at £70,000. With rules, regulations and laws – the late nineteenth century abounded in associations and federations, all under zealous gentlemanly control – came dress codes. J. A. Mangan in his invaluable *Athleticism in the Victorian and Edwardian Public School* reproduces four photographs of the Harrow cricket XI over a fifty-year period. The 1862 team carries informality to the point of negligence: the players lounge at odd angles or lie sprawled on the ground. By 1876 the atmosphere is still studiously casual: the occasional bat dangles here and there amid a backdrop of open-necked shirts and grimy trousers. In the 1910 photograph, on the other hand, eleven immaculately togged exquisites – capped, bescarved and white-blazered – sit in a symmetrical phalanx. The effect is faintly ominous: martial, even. They could almost be a bodyguard, a hit squad, a warlord's retinue. A flag emblazoned with a rampant lion hangs in the background. It is practically a battle standard.

The symbolism of this sporting choreography, its poise, precision and intent, is inescapable. It is also profoundly ironic. The Victorian amateur who looked down his nose at a professional sportsman for not regarding games playing as an end in itself could hardly have failed to notice that his own attitude to sport was deeply compromised. By the end of the nineteenth century the original Victorian moral project of Godliness and Good Learning had become thoroughly debased, turned at its lower echelons into a straightforward justification of athletic prowess. At the most basic level this involved the mass importation of sporting meta-phors into the moral framework. The game of life. God the eternal scorer. The umpire passing judge-ment. According to Eustace Miles, author of *Let's Play the Game: Or the Anglo-Saxon Sporting Spirit* (1904), human weaknesses were merely 'the balls that bowl most of us in daily life'. If we were unable to remain free of sin, it was because 'we have taken our eye off the ball'.

It would be odd, given the destinies of most

Victorian public school boys, if all this high moral purpose were to lack an Imperial connection. Robert Baden-Powell, founder of the Boy Scout movement, exhorted his youthful audience: 'Don't be disgraced like the young Romans, who lost the Empire of their forefathers by being wishy-washer slackers without any go or patriotism. Play up. Each man in his place and play the game.' Life, the captain informs 'Baxter', the hero of an anonymous late Victorian allegory, *Baxter's Second Innings*, is simply a cricket match, in which each player has three wickets – Truth, Honour and Purity – to defend against the demon fast bowler Temptation. Underlying these exhortations lay the cheering assumption that moral worth could be obtained by a kind of osmosis, merely by picking up bat, ball or racket. As one contemporary homilist, T. L. Papillon put it:

> Many a lad who leaves an English public school disgracefully ignorant of the rudiments of useful knowledge, who can speak no language but his own, and writes that imperfectly, to whom the noble literature of his country and the stirring history of his forefathers are almost a sealed book, and who has devoted a great part of his time and nearly all his thoughts to athletic sports, yet brings away with him something beyond all price, a manly straightforward character, a scorn of lying and meanness, habits of obedience and command and reckless courage. Thus

equipped, he goes out into the world, and bears a man's part in subduing the earth, taming its wild folk, and building up the Empire.

Even Strickland, as the Havenhall headmaster readily concedes – 'never was – I know he will pardon me for saying it – a good bookman'. More enlightened public school heads – F. W. Farrar, for example, at Marlborough – might complain about 'extravagant athleticism', but these were isolated voices far back in the mid-Victorian mix. It takes only a glance at the average novel of public school life, with its relish of 'hard knocks' and routine disparagements of intellect, to establish quite how deep into the nineteenth-century consciousness the cult of games-playing manliness was to penetrate.

Meanwhile, several rungs beneath this empyrean of moral propaganda and Christian good fellowship, dramatic changes were beginning to affect the way in which soccer – as football was about to be renamed – was played, and the number and character of the spectators who watched it. Rather to their surprise, and certainly against their inclinations, the public school sportsmen who administered the game found that by the twilight of the Victorian era they had acquired the one thing liable to wrest the game from the hands of the people who had effectively created it – a mass audience.

The Football Association, born in 1863 out of a desire to establish a proper rule book after centuries of cheery extemporising, bore all the hallmarks of the Victorian sporting association. This is to say that it was conceived by gentlemen – each of the founding clubs consisted of ex-public school boys and was based in the south of England – and its ambitions were largely regulatory, confined in the main to codes, conduct and protocol. Its amateurism was *ipso facto*, if only for the reason that there was at this time in England hardly such a thing as a footballer who was paid for his appearances. Within a decade, the Association had a challenge cup, inaugurally secured by Wanderers, a famous Old Boys' side, with a 1-0 victory against the Royal Engineers. It took another decade for anyone beyond the catchment area of the southern public schools to breach this citadel, when Blackburn Olympic saw off the Old Etonians. And yet the final of 1883 was a landmark in footballing history – the last time that an amateur team, or a team of ex-public school boys from the south of England bore off a trophy that, the FA's accounts show, took all of £20 to commission.

In the next three seasons another Blackburn side – Rovers – won the cup three times running, on the last occasion watched by 15,000 people, five times the audience of the original final. The days of good-humoured friendlies conducted by bands of mustachioed army subalterns and bachelor dons on boundaryless pitches watched by a handful of cognoscenti had passed. In their place marched a procession of northern working-class sides, based on factory, foundry or working-men's club whose progress around the country was trailed by thousands of fiercely patriotic local supporters.

To most contemporary onlookers, the growth of mass-participation working-class soccer could be instantly marked down as one of Carlyle's Regrettable Modern Tendencies. The ecclesiastical historian David Newsome, examining the question of late Victorian church attendance, suggests that 'the greatest threat of all was the diversion offered to all classes, and the lower classes most of all, by the advent of professional football. This is what the working man regarded as the highlight of his weekend.' To many representatives of the different Victorian churches, Newsome concludes, it seemed as if the passion engendered by football was rapidly becoming the working man's religion. There were practical explanations for this access of enthusiasm. By the 1880s a succession of Factory Acts had established the principle of the Saturday half-day. The national railway network was on the one hand more extensive and on the other more affordable. To the Lancashire mill-hand of Dickens's day a trip to London counted as an unheard-of luxury. By the

1890s the football crowd, rapt and enthusiastic, streaming across the platforms of mainline stations in search of match-day 'specials', was a regular part of weekend urban life.

One inexorable consequence of this explosion of bumper crowds, charter trains and newspaper 'sporting finals' – all the paraphernalia we now associate with a game gone big-league and prime-time – was a change in the complexion of the people who played it. In the great majority of cases, the amateur teams which turned out on public parks and heaths disdained to levy contributions from the handfuls of spectators who congregated on their touchlines. To the works committees and local businessmen who presided over the triumphs of the first big northern sides, on the other hand, com-merce would always be a factor in the administrative equation. Pitches had to be hired. As the volume of spectators increased, grandstands and enclosures had to be built to accommodate them. More important still, to justify their sponsors' expenditure, the team was expected to win. To do that it needed the best players available; scintillating new talent of this type would need payment, if only in kind.

The covert semi-professionalism of the northern game was first brought to public notice in the late 1870s when two members of the Darwen side competing in the FA Cup were revealed as imported

Scotsmen lured south by the promise of well-paid, part-time jobs at a local cotton mill. Twenty or even ten years before, the Darwen scandal and others like it might have resulted in a standoff between the amateur die-hards of the FA Committee and northern newcomers who were quite prepared to form a breakaway group. By this stage, though, there was an inevitability about professionalism's advance: fearful of diminished influence, the FA backed down. By 1885, the year in which Blackburn Rovers won their second FA Cup and only six years since the exposure of the Darwen shamateurs, professionalism was legal. By the 1890s, by which time there was a Football League with two divisions and twenty-four clubs, not one of them amateur or hailing from anywhere south of the Midlands, it was a way of life.

The ironies of this thirty-year transformation were rarely lost on those amateur sides which had previously regarded the FA Cup as, if not their private fiefdom, then an arena in which their qualities of selflessness and team spirit could be displayed to advantage. The public schools and their old boys had effectively created the modern game, only to have it snatched from their grasp by an upstart northern horde (the origins of several of the northern sides, founded by gentlemanly sponsors and sporting clerics, could now be seen as a dreadful

Trojan Horse). Where had the competitive ethic, sporting protocol and patriotic fervour taken root, if not on the playing fields of Eton, Harrow and Winchester? Questions of this kind were regularly debated among amateur sporting men in the early 1880s, and doubtless some of the people debating them were present at the meeting, held in the early months of the 1881–2 season, which brought the greatest amateur team in English football into existence.

Given the wider socio-cultural background, it is tempting to see the birth of the Corinthians as a deliberate rearguard action in the fight against professionalism – neatly enough, the motivating spirit turns out to have been N. L. Jackson, the FA's assistant honorary secretary – and yet the stated object was the restoration of national sporting pride. Scottish teams playing in international matches were adjudged to be superior performers as they had more opportunities to play together. It was time for English sides to catch up. A better hint of the founders' intentions could be found in the club constitution of 1883, which declared that its players 'shall not compete for any challenge cup or any prize of any description'. This hard-line prohibition was later amended to allow appearances in the Sheriff of London's Charity Shield – a charitable institution – but the absolutist note remained. Any lessons on how to play the game would be dealt out in friendly matches, the *locus classicus* of the amateur ethic.

In less purposeful hands the project might easily have degenerated into a period freak: one of those innumerable mixed bicycling clubs and Settes of Odde Volumes in which the Victorian age abounded. As it was, within three years of their foundation the Corinthians had metamorphosed into the pre-eminent amateur side in the kingdom. Given the limited resources at their disposal – all the pitches were borrowed or hired and the enterprise was self-financing – the club's achievements in its first few years of existence were quite without parallel.

There is a wonderful moment in *How Steeple Sinderby Wanderers Won the FA Cup* in which the Cup victories of the captain's report come jumbled up with more routine Saturday afternoon engagements ('Mr Slingsby (capt.), reporting on *Interim Progress*, stated that his team had defeated Hackthorn Young Conservatives (away) 13-0, N. Baddesley Congs Tennis & Football Club (home) 14-0, Bennington British Rail (away) 12-0 and Aston Villa (at Wolverhampton) 2-1. The chairman commented favourably on these statistics.'). Corinthians meetings must have gone much the same way. In the 1884–5 season, for example, they beat the FA Cup holders Blackburn Rovers twice, as

well as administering two defeats to the other
leading Lancashire side, Preston North End.

International recognition soon followed. The
club historian estimated that between 1881 and
1906 a third of all places in England's fixtures
against Scotland were taken by Corinthians players.
The matches against Wales in 1894 and 1898 were
effectively contested by Corinthians XIs. No doubt
this record owed something to the bias of the FA's
amateur-friendly selectors, but the fact remains that
for a period of nearly twenty years, deep into the
Edwardian era, the Corinthians could take on and
beat any respectable side in England. As late as 1904
they annihilated Bury, the FA Cup holders, 10-3;
the following year brought a 7-1 savaging of First
Division Aston Villa.

How did they do it? The obvious explanation is
gestational. Soccer was still in embryo. The complex
calibrations of technical pizzazz and superior tactics
that allow a Ferguson or a Mourinho to go on
winning week in, week out, had simply yet to be
developed. The Hon. Walter de Toffe, let us say, an
Old Carthusian recently embarked on a career at the
Board of Trade and turning out for weekly practice
sessions at Richmond Park in the company of his
former school chums, was liable to be quite as
accomplished as ex-foundryman Harry Hardcastle,
lately elevated to the playing staff of Accrington

Stanley. Better accomplished in the majority of cases, as the physical differentiation consequent upon class status was more pronounced in the late nineteenth century. In the average north of England mining village, five feet nine inches was a very respectable height. In the eleven-strong list of additions to the Woolwich Arsenal side during the 1891–2 season, not a man was taller than five feet ten and a half, and Mackay, the Scottish centre-half, was under five feet five.

However pronounced this physical superiority may have been, the proponents of the amateur game knew that its advantages went only so far, that there were great areas of sporting prowess where it scarcely penetrated. The Corinthians, to put it starkly, believed that their distinction was innate; that it derived from the kind of people they were and the attitude with which they approached the game, came, in fact, from an ethic that in the end had very little to do with sport at all.

Formal statements of the Corinthian credo bear this out. In 1906, to celebrate its quarter-century, the club sanctioned an official history. Even by the Olympian standards of the age, *Annals of the Corinthian Football Club* is an impressive production. B. O. Corbett, the volume's compiler, furnishes the 'Story of the Corinthians'. The great amateur cricketer and athlete C. B. Fry supplies character

sketches of leading players. There are modest
résumés from the gazetteer of overseas tours – the
1893 excursion to South Africa, let us say, when the
team called on President Kruger ('After talking some
time on general topics he wished us all a good time,
and we departed, little dreaming, perhaps, that the
world would soon be ringing with his name') before
vanquishing a local side 21-2. In 'Hints on the Game'
T. S. Rowlandson offers advice on goalkeeping ('The
lot of a goal-keeper may not be considered the most
enviable on the field, and it is certainly one of the
most nerve-trying') while B. Middleditch dilates on
'How to play half-back' ('. . . don't make it obvious
to whom you are going to pass', etc). But the *Annals*
is more than a scrapbook of doughty deeds and the
exploits of such larger than life characters as 'Nuts'
Cobbold ('the Bayard of the football field, the
forward without fear and without blame', etc) or
E. C. Bambridge, known as 'Charlie Bam', who
having broken his leg some weeks before a crucial
match outfoxed his opponents by turning up with a
shin guard covering the sound limb and scoring the
winning goal. At its heart lies both a defence and an
exposition of the amateur game.

Mindful of the specimen Edwardian headmaster,
who had already begun to shake his head over
'sporting mania', the editor begins by acknowledg-
ing the 'abuse of athletics'. However, he is

'convinced of their value when rightly used; and it is just because, in his opinion, the Corinthians are working in the best interests of sport, that he has presumed to collect a few facts about their history'. There are, apparently, 'some special considerations to be urged in connection with the Corinthians which appear to the writer to warrant some record of their doings'. The Corinthians' *raison d'être* turns out to have three aspects. On the one hand, its members are 'Missionaries of Empire': the club 'has played no inconsiderable part in helping to bring the Colonies and the Mother Country closer together' (as for the tours of non-Imperial countries, these have 'done much to popularise the British idea of true sportsmanship'). At the same time the club 'is always ready to aid charitable objects, although it is not suggested that it claims a monopoly in this respect'. Finally, and distinct from the Imperial project though necessarily connected to it, there is the insistence that a game should be a game. 'The Corinthians have, from the first, set their faces against "pot-hunting".' With the single exception of the Sheriff of London's Charity Shield, 'the club is not allowed by its rules to enter for any competition'. This is 'a valuable protest against the growing tendency to play the game only for the prizes it will bring'.

And how was the game to be played? Much is

made, here and in the match reports, of the Corinthians' manner of playing: 'a style of their own'; 'one only has to watch a Corinthian eleven play a professional side at the present time to notice the difference of style'. Contemporary evidence suggests that the club did indeed cultivate its own distinctive tactics: they were much lauded among the game's cognoscenti for the forward pass executed on the run, or what was known as 'the sweeping method of progression'. And yet, equally clearly, something more fundamental was at stake.

> The excellence of professional play generally gives the impression that the many tricks and intricacies of the game are mastered by mechanical ability and laborious training. But the passes of the amateur, though made as often and as accurately, appear to be the result rather of natural instinct. The amateur is essentially independent in his methods, and it is this individualism, combined with his public school training, which makes his style of play so distinctive.

On the other hand, this individualism was always secondary to the best interests of the team. As Gilbert Smith, a prep school teacher who turned out for the Corinthians for twenty years, wrote in a late Victorian instructional guide:

The great object of forwards should be to work together with the precision of a machine, and that the individual credit of anyone should be subservient to the good of the side. A selfish player, however brilliant, should never be allowed to remain in any team – he seeks for self glorification rather than the good of his side.

The gap between Blackburn Rovers and 'Nuts' Cobbold, 'Charlie Bam' and Co. was not merely technical, it was *moral*: not achieved through practice or adherence to a system of play but by a state of mind. A finely judged state of mind, too, which required one to try hard, but not too hard, or rather to exert oneself without seeming to, to display poise, character and good comradeship rather than doggedness, muscle and self-interest. Winning was fine, but not making a fuss about winning, or losing, was finer still. Worse, for anyone who aspired to this Olympian state of impartiality, even temper and sang-froid, although such qualities could be encouraged in the non-amateur, their essence was pre-ordained. An amateur, to put it starkly, was born; a professional made. The discerning onlooker preferred nature to nurture.

This tocsin and its subsidiary peals clang on endlessly through *Annals of the Corinthian Football Club*. C. B. Fry notes that the fortunes of professional clubs are inextricably mixed up with business, to the point where whoever undertakes the commercial management has more to do with sporting success than the actual players. 'None of these things, however, come into Corinthian history. The club has never possessed a ground of its own, and has never had to consider finance. Its story is the story of its great players, pure and simple.' Meanwhile, the foreign tours kept coming – South Africa, again, in 1903, where eight thousand spectators turned out to watch a match against a Western Provinces XI; Hungary in 1904, where, after the 27-0 despatch of a local side, the Corinthians captain consoled his defeated opponents with the assurance that 'if . . . they were ready to take a beating in a thoroughly sportsmanlike manner, they were also ready to take a few hints from a team with far greater experience of the game . . .'; Scandinavia in the same year.

Pace C. B. Fry, much of this endeavour was propagandist – Hungary, for example, was promising territory for an amateur team as 'so far professionalism has been avoided, and such a thing as a professional team seems to be, as far as Hungary is concerned, relegated to a very distant future' – but it was not in any way exclusive. Playing professional sides on their home grounds beyond the Trent, the Corinthians were keen to fraternise with local supporters. One of the virtues Fry ascribes to

'Charlie Bam', it transpires, was his appeal to the
working classes: 'his northern admirers, whether
they were the keen mill-hands of Preston or the dry
shipwrights of Glasgow, were always waiting to give
him a hearty handshake.' If there was a political
agenda lurking beneath this tide of good fellowship
and clasped hands, it was an inclusive, patriarchal,
One-Nation Toryism.

Charlie Bam and crowds of deferential mill-hands
excepted, the Golden Age was dwindling to a close.
So fleeting are its true dimensions, in fact, that
'golden age' is a serious misnomer. The professionals
were catching up. By the turn of the twentieth
century only a single amateur remained in the
England team. Although *Annals of the Corinthian
Football Club* understandably chooses not to pro-
claim the fact, its trumpeting of the foreign tour and
international goodwill side of the club's activities
was a way of glozing over a radically diminished
local prestige. The steady expansion of the professional game assisted this marginalising process.
As the *Annals* historian noted, apropos the cessation
of fixtures with Preston North End, 'Of late years,
owing to the extension of the League, which makes
it harder, season by season, to arrange friendly
matches with the big professional teams, no meeting
between the clubs has taken place.' Victories against
league clubs – there was an 11-3 thrashing of

Manchester United – were invariably tarnished by the professionals' habit of fielding what were essentially reserve teams.

More important even than this was what might be called an imaginative lapse, the inability of a middle-class amateur establishment to grasp the point of professional sport, the aspirations that it symbolised and the – occasionally bitter – passions that it roused. The roots of this divide, inevitably, lie somewhere in class, but there was also a cultural severance, born out of the failure of an establishment culture to understand the nature, and the appeal, of this effervescent popular alternative. Curiously enough, most of its symptoms can be found in the mind of a writer who has some claims to be regarded as the greatest cultural critic of the entire twentieth century: George Orwell.

VI

'True Cricketers'

As the Eton-educated son of a mid-ranking colonial civil servant, Orwell's attitude to 'games' was thoroughly representative of his time. An enthusiastic prep school footballer – there is a letter home to his mother which records his playing in goal while the opposing forwards 'ran at me like angry dogs' – his solitary sporting achievement as a teenager was to score a goal in the Eton Wall Game of St Andrew's Day 1921. In fact the only surviving film footage of Eric Blair, to use his real name, consists of a few shaky frames, courtesy of the Pathé cameraman who covered the match, in which a loping figure, swathed in jerseys and outsize scarves, parades across a playing field with his team-mates.

Later, as an assistant superintendent in the Burma Police, he took part in soccer matches between police sides and teams of native Burmans. Intended to promote fraternisation between conqueror and subject race these, as he notes in the essay 'Shooting an Elephant', were a heaven-sent opportunity for score-settling. 'As a police officer I was an obvious target and was baited whenever it seemed safe to do so. When a nimble Burman tripped me up on the football field and the referee (another Burman) looked the other way, the crowd yelled with hideous laughter.'

As in practically everything Orwell wrote about his time in Burma, one sees his instincts tugging him both ways. On the one hand, as a paid-up anti-Imperialist, he sympathises with the Burmans and their subjugation at the hands of a declining Raj. On the other his sense of fair play is continually out-raged. As he notes in the same essay, 'With one part of my mind I thought of the British Raj as an unbreakable tyranny, something clamped down, *in saecula saeculorum*, upon the will of subject peoples; with another part I thought the greatest joy would be to drive a bayonet into a Buddhist priest's guts.' Essentially Orwell shipped with him to the East a moral code that could have been lifted wholesale from *Strickland of the Sixth*: his real complaint about being upended on a Burmese football pitch, you feel, is that the culprit is not 'playing the game'.

In later life Orwell took no great interest in sport. Swimming in the sea off Southwold or taking his fiancée, Eileen O'Shaughnessy, out riding at Greenwich was about the limit of his athletic pursuits, although he seems to have been mildly fixated on the annual Eton versus Harrow match at Lord's, to which several of his letters and diary entries from the late 1930s refer. By chance, in June 1940 his Home Guard duties took him to a conference held in the committee room at Lord's. Orwell was suitably awed:

> Last time I was at Lord's must have been at the Eton–Harrow match in 1921. At that time I should have felt that to go into the Pavilion, not being a member of the M.C.C., was on a par with pissing on the altar, and years later would have had some vague idea that it was a legal offence for which you could be prosecuted.

Set against these almost sacerdotal musings about cricket and the sanctity of its administrative HQ, his indifference to the most popular national pastime can occasionally seem rather odd. His brother-in-law Humphrey Dakin's criticism of the notably gloomy reportage of northern working-class life in *The Road to Wigan Pier* (1937) was that, 'What he describes is accurate. But it's only half, it's the depressing half. He didn't go to any of the football matches where they were enjoying themselves.'

And yet, towards the end of his life – he died in 1950 – Orwell did produce two essays which have some bearing on sporting questions. The first, written in the winter of 1945 for the left-wing

weekly magazine *Tribune*, reflects on the four
exhibition matches played in the UK by the touring
Moscow Dynamo XI. Although intended (rather
like the police games in Burma) to foster a
cooperative spirit of post-war amity, these had been
notably ill-tempered: in the game at Highbury
several players had come to blows. Orwell diagnosed
an exercise in disguised nationalism. 'Nearly all the
sports practised nowadays are competitive', he
pronounced. 'You play to win, and the game has
little meaning unless you do your utmost to win.'

Competitive pressures were bad enough in
England. In 'young countries', where both games
playing and nationalism were comparatively recent
developments, their influence was deeply corrosive.
The Burmese games of his youth, he recalled, had
been marred by crowd trouble; '. . . I have seen the
supporters of one side break through the police and
disable the goalkeeper of the opposing side at a
critical moment.' Once feelings of rivalry were
aroused in a sporting contest, he deduced, any idea
of playing by the rules disappeared. Instead the
participants '. . . forget that victory gained through
cheating or through the intervention of the crowd is
meaningless'.

Here again, one sees how much the Victorian
sporting ethos had contributed to Orwell's moral
thinking (as a teenager, he records elsewhere, he had

been profoundly shocked at a village cricket match when the local squire countermanded an umpiring decision). To a man reared on the playing fields of Eton, contemporary sporting arrangements were morally disgusting. 'Serious sport has nothing to do with fair play. It is bound up with hatred, jealousy, boastfulness, disregard of all rules and sadistic pleasure in witnessing violence: in other words it is war minus the shooting.' Going back to the immediate spectacle of 'young men kicking each other' at Hampden Park and Highbury, he concludes, 'There cannot be much doubt that the whole thing is bound up with the rise of nationalism – that is, with the lunatic modern habit of identifying oneself with large power units and seeing everything in terms of competitive prestige.'

Naturally there are points to be made in Orwell's favour. Even as a child of five monitoring my father's reaction to the 1966 World Cup final I had an idea that the Second World War was being figuratively refought here in our front room. All the same, it is odd that Orwell, so sane and sympathetic on most aspects of working-class life, cannot see that for the average twenty-something who played the game professionally in the 1940s, association football was one of the very few means of working-class self-advancement available, a hotly coveted step-up from the factory floor, the foundry or in some cases even the slum. (A minor step, given the sums of money available, but highly desirable in the context of the average working-class life.) Orwell's essays are full of admiration for 'ordinary people' who by dint of scholarships and self-determination clamber their way up from the backstreets – 'the finest type of man I know'. Less intellectual types, he might have reflected, could only do it with their feet. Neither, as *Tribune* readers were quick to assure him, was the average footballing crowd made up of sinister, blood-lusting über-patriots. As a Mr E. S. Fayers of Harrow pointed out in the magazine's letters' page a fortnight later:

> As to the spectators, with the greatest possible diffidence, I suggest that George is in danger of falling into the error of intellectual contempt for the 'mob'. These football crowds, if only he got among them, he would find are not great ignorant mobs of sadistic morons. They are a pretty good mixture of just ordinary men. A little puzzled, a little anxious, steady, sceptical, humorous, knowledgeable, having a little fun, hoping for a bit of excitement and definitely getting quite a lot of enjoyment out of that glorious king of games – football.

It is E. M. Forster's point all over again: only connect.

Orwell's other significant contribution to sporting literature is a review written for the *Manchester Evening News* eighteen months earlier of Edmund Blunden's *Cricket Country*. Cricket, it should be pointed out, was an essential component of the kind of English literary life now generally stigmatised by the adjective 'Georgian'. 'Authors' XIs' were a staple of the amateur fixture lists and a full-length novel – A. G. Macdonnell's *England, Their England* (1933) – was contrived around the adventures of J. C. Squire's 'Invalids' touring side. With certain exceptions, the writers involved in these leisurely tours of Home Counties villages were not of a kind that Orwell admired – their compound of briar pipes, beer-drinking and 'Sussex by the Sea' was not to his taste – and yet his praise of *Cricket Country* is quite unfeigned. He begins by mounting a defence of cricket against its 'demonisation' by left-wing critics who erroneously imagine that it is played chiefly by the rich. In fact the reverse is the case: with twenty-two players, two umpires and a scorer, the game offers plenty of opportunities for social interaction. 'Contrary to what its detractors say, cricket is not an inherently snobbish game.' Edmund Blunden, he quickly decides, is 'a true cricketer', the test of a true cricketer being 'that he shall prefer village cricket to good cricket'. The author may remember Ranjitsinhji playing his famous leg-glide, yet

It is obvious that all his friendliest memories are of village cricket . . . the informal village game, where everyone plays in braces, where the blacksmith is liable to be called away in mid-innings on an urgent job, and sometimes, about the time when the light begins to fade, a ball driven for four kills a rabbit on the boundary.

It quickly becomes clear that, just as professional football awakens all Orwell's worst fears about nationalism, so amateur cricket stokes up some of his most deeply felt emotions about Englishness; in the end the rustic cricketers on their undulating square are less important than the atmosphere that envelopes them. Significantly, Orwell goes on to note that 'in his love of cricket, Mr Blunden is in good literary company'. There follows a roll call of cricket-fancying writers, which includes Byron, Keats, Cowper and Trollope, and a lament for the world smashed to pieces by the events of 1914–18, which Orwell imagines to be the great climacteric of Blunden's life. 'The war shattered the leisurely world he had known, and, as he sadly perceives, cricket has never been quite the same since.' Nostalgia for a lost, prelapsarian cricketing paradise endured deep into the twentieth century. In the final volume of *The Lyttelton–Hart-Davis Letters* – correspondence exchanged in the late 1950s between a retired Eton master and one of his former pupils – George

Lyttelton elegises a hero of his Edwardian youth:

> You probably never saw Reggie Spooner bat. You
> would not have forgotten it – the purest champagne.
> Even bowlers enjoyed his punishment of them – the
> lovely grace of the stroke itself – and the courtesy, so
> kindly without anything remotely condescending. It
> was Colin Blythe who after being despatched
> through the covers said to him, 'Mr Spooner, I
> would give all my bowling to make a shot like that.'
> Trueman would not have said that.

To which one rather wants to yell out that
Trueman, a no-nonsense Yorkshireman with a living
to make, was effectively being paid for the number
of wickets he took. The same point – *mutatis
mutandis* – applies to Orwell's young men kicking
each other's shins at Hampden Park.

VII

'Mr Sheppard to You'

Looking at one or two of the cheerier productions of inter-war cricketing literature – *England, Their England*, perhaps, or Hugh de Selincourt's *The Cricket Match* (1924) – one might be forgiven for assuming that Orwell's obituary for village cricket was a panegyric preached over an empty grave. All the same, scarcely a single major British sport emerged from the Great War with its founding principles intact: seen in the round, the inter-war era soon declares itself as a series of attritional skirmishes between professionals and amateurs, in which professionalism, occasional checks notwithstanding, was always going to have the upper hand.

There were two main explanations for this superiority. The first was the dramatic effect wrought by the war on the young middle-to-upper-middle-class population. Most of the public school old boys' sides had been cut to ribbons in the Flanders mud. First-class cricketing counties seeking to replenish their squads on pre-1914 lines rapidly conceded defeat: there were simply not enough Oxbridge blues and promising public school bats to go round.

The second reason was more fundamental. Here in a mass-industrial age, the measure of a sport's success, by and large, was the size of the audience it attracted. The money that this audience was prepared to pay to watch the sport simultaneously inflated the rewards available to the people who played it and enhanced the level of competition. To stand aside from the commercialising process was to risk exclusion from the sport's future: the best prizes, the keenest fans, the biggest audiences, lay elsewhere. Publishing his autobiography in 1934, at a time when the Wimbledon championship was still open only to amateurs, the future three-times men's singles champion Fred Perry inserted a chapter headed 'The Case for Professionalism', in which he argued the futility of staging a tournament in which half a dozen of the world's best players were ineligible to compete. 'Either let tennis revert to its old pleasant position as a spare time occupation for its exponents, with less efficiency but no less fun; or let the nations' rackets, whether plied by amateur or professional, follow the sun increasingly from continent to continent.' There was no feasible middle course, Perry argued: the pursuit of excellence demanded a free market. A mere thirty-four years later, the Wimbledon establishment acceded.

From the angle of the sports historian, Perry is a highly symbolic figure: a product of the council school and the municipal parks, who was thought – not least by his Labour MP father – to have opened up a new entry route into the game. 'My son Fred's progress in lawn tennis was rapid and may be unusual', the Member for Kettering enthused. 'It has been by way of the organised games at elementary and secondary schools, and later through the channels of the lawn tennis clubs, rather than a university.'

More to the point, perhaps, Perry's amateurism – like that of many 'amateur' cricketers – was deeply suspect. His career on the international circuit was subsidised by his father, a point on which *My Story* is winningly candid ('If anyone sent abroad, with expenses paid, to represent his country in any sport is a 'shamateur' then the country abounds in them and they are not confined to tennis.'). Perry's tense relationship with the tennis authorities – he turned pro after his Wimbledon triumphs – and indeed with the Wimbledon crowds (who, he maintained, had never really seen an Englishman of his era who didn't like to lose) had echoes elsewhere across the sporting firmament.

The period 1918–39 was characterised by the efforts of predominantly middle-class administrative bodies – the MCC, the Lawn Tennis Association, the Amateur Athletics Association – to keep professional excesses in check. The tenacity with which they stuck to this long rearguard action should not be underestimated, and in at least two sports they were completely successful. Rowing, for example, which in the nineteenth century had been a popular working-class pastime with a strong betting element, was by the 1920s firmly under the control of the Henley establishment. The same defence of ancient principle was brought to track and field athletics. Joe Darby, the great professional long-jumper, who used a system of hand-held weights to assist his passage over rivers, had been a household name in the mid-Victorian era. A representative British athlete of the 1920s was Lord Burghley, who competed in the 1924 Olympics while still an undergraduate at Magdalene College, Cambridge.

With the exception of some of the northern road races, athletics had never been a mass-spectator sport. Cricket was an altogether different proposition. Here, as in tennis, lavish financial rewards were now on offer beyond the margins of the official game. North of England league cricket, for instance, attracted five-figure gates and large working-class memberships. Most players were amateurs, but the increasingly solid financing of the leagues occasionally allowed for extravagant gestures. In

1922 the Lancashire town of Nelson hired the Australian fast bowler Ted McDougall on a salary of £700 per annum; seven years later they laid out a reputed £1000 to secure the services of the West Indian Learie Constantine.

The first-class game, meanwhile, maintained an occasionally precarious balance between predominantly public school and university-trained southerners and dour northern journeymen. The proportion of amateurs among the ranks of first-class cricketers in the 1930s has been put at around 40 per cent. On the other hand, of the twenty-one county championships contested between 1918 and 1939 twelve were won by Yorkshire and five by their arch-rivals Lancashire. In each case the team consisted of ten professionals led by an amateur captain.

The near universal professionalism of county cricket north of the Trent is deceptive: control of the game remained in strictly amateur hands. The great West Indian writer C. L. R. James characterised the 1920s as a period of slow yet inexorable decline in amateur influence. This is accurate, but it ignores the unrelenting grip of Lord Harris, Treasurer of the MCC from 1916 to 1931, or the famously obstructive Yorkshire chairman Lord Hawke, who remarked in 1925: 'Pray God no professional may ever captain England . . . If the time comes when we are to have no more amateurs captaining England, well I don't say England will become exactly like league football, but it will be a thousand pities and will not be good for the game.' Domineering old-style administrators of the Harris/Hawke vintage were capable of exerting a profound influence on the upper reaches of the game. Not one professional cricketer captained England between 1918 and 1939. But over a third of the forty-seven amateur internationals did so.

Inevitably, these distinctions were reflected at the basic, workaday level at which the game was played. Rather a lot has been written about the social demarcations of inter-war first-class cricket, its 'Gentleman' and 'Player' divides and its segregated accommodation, a kind of lower-rung apartheid that extended even to separate entrances on to the playing area. Certainly these divisions existed. The England spin bowler Fred Rust remembered being ordered back to the nets by a Middlesex gauleiter with the reminder that 'You are nothing more or less than a hired labourer in the game'. A professional at large in the first-class game in the era of Stanley Baldwin could expect to be referred to in the match programme by his surname and, if on tour, stay in a separate hotel. Patsy Hendren, the solitary pro-fessional selected for the MCC against Australia in 1934, made his way on to the pitch in splendid isolation from his ten amateur colleagues. All nonsense, of course, and antiquated class-bound prejudice from the days of top hats and morning coats, and yet it is possible to exaggerate the adversarial nature of the inter-war game.

No doubt there were officious amateur captains. As late as the early fifties Tom Graveney, congratulating the amateur David Sheppard on a century and addressing him as 'David', was instantly ticked off by the Gloucester captain Basil Allen: 'He's Mr Sheppard to you.' Officialdom, too, frequently went out of its way to foster the resentments of the Rust-era ingrate. Frank Lea, the Middlesex professional opener, for example, was once hauled into the office of the secretary, Sir Francis Lacy, and asked why, having been given out lbw, he had appeared to hesitate when leaving the field. Lea explained that he had stopped to retrieve a fragment of his bat smashed off by the ball. He was sternly rebuked and warned that he would be dismissed if he repeated the offence.

Most professionals, on the other hand, diagnosed an archaic survival which, if occasionally irksome, rarely affected their ability to prosper in the game. As Dennis Compton, who began his professional career in 1936, put it, 'People today would say "How humiliating, coming out of different entrances" but it wasn't so.' Even the predatory Lord

Hawke turns out to have been misrepresented. Curiously, reproductions of the parenthesised speech quoted above nearly always omit the crucial words 'I love professionals, every one of them, but we have always had an amateur skipper.'* Lord Hawke was capable of discreet – or not so discreet – interference in pursuit of this desirable aim: Herbert Sutcliffe, elected Yorkshire's first professional captain in 1928, was quietly induced to withdraw his candidature. Yet many professionals relished the independence that an amateur captain could bring to a predominantly professional team. When it came to captaincy, the Yorkshire firebrand Fred Trueman observed, albeit at a slightly later date, 'There was no doubt in my mind that the independence of the amateur who was willing to speak up for his team and if necessary to take on the County Committee was the best combination we ever had.'

As in football, though, the amateur/professional distinctions were those of style, background, *élan*. If the definition of a true amateur was someone who could afford to play first-class cricket without financial support of any kind, then barely a dozen members of the thirties cricketing establishment were amateurs in any meaningful sense. In the last

*See, for example, Ross McKibbin, *Cultures and Classes: England 1918–1951* (1998), p. 335.

resort almost everybody got paid, whether the money came from a sinecure in the club's back office or by way of heavily massaged expense claims. Nigel Haig, appointed Middlesex captain in 1929, needed not only the backing of Lord Harris – who, for good measure, was his uncle – but the promise of financial support. Wally Hammond, then a professional, reverted to amateur status when he was offered a job by the Marshall tyre company: this not only gave him a bigger salary but brought the England captaincy within his sights. Much of this employment, if it came to that, was discreetly provided by the clubs themselves, in the shape of assistant secretaryships. However valiantly Lord Harris and his associates might strive to keep up a pretence of genuine amateurism, the reality was sharply apparent to anyone who took an informed interest in the game. Looking back at the final inter-war season from the vantage point of 1943, the editor of *Wisden* noted, 'There still existed in county cricket a few, a very few, amateurs who earned no money, directly or indirectly, from the game. They received only their travelling and hotel expenses, and in some cases, not even that . . . But they were survivors of a lost society that was nearly gone.'

Ambiguities of this kind were not exclusive to cricket: they affected nearly every major sport of the inter-war years. And they extended even to football, where the professional tide had long since swept away such frail defences as the amateur game had cared to throw up in its retreating wake. Except for a few part-timers in the lower reaches of the league, club playing staffs were uniformly professional. The Football Association, on the other hand, took most of its representatives from the amateur-dominated county bodies. Club directors – the point is made time and again in memoirs of the period – tended to be local 'worthies', city elders and sporting business-men, anxious to keep a grip on their investment, socially distinct from the players, keen to minimise the running costs of the operation.

Several factors worked to suppress a free market in football, but by far the most important was an earnings cap. Even with the help of sponsorship deals, First Division footballers struggled to evade the constraints of the maximum wage: the England centre-forward Tommy Lawton earned a modest £531 in 1939, at a time when a City clerk might have taken home £200 a year. Although resented by the leading players, the maximum wage was loyally upheld by the clubs and quite a few lower-league performers on the not entirely spurious grounds that it distributed talent evenly through the game and was a way of supporting the medium-grade player. Depending on your point of view and the position you occupied in the game, it was either an indefensible restraint on trade, or an attempt to maintain some vestige of a level playing field, in which a club's success was not wholly dependent on its cash resources. Despite a certain amount of agitation, the average professional footballer's weekly wage in the 1930s was between £6 and £7: worth having (for purposes of comparison my father's salary when he started work at the Norwich Union Insurance Company in 1937 was £45 a year) but well below the standard middle-class income scale.

The people who administered soccer had known at an early stage that large-scale professionalism was inevitable. By coming to terms with it they contrived to minimise its impact. At its lower levels, in any case, the game was still run on a shoestring and in an atmosphere of homely communality. On match days in Norwich in the 1920s the players walked to the ground with the crowd. The assistant trainer's wife washed the team kit in her kitchen copper while her seven-year-old son officiated as club mascot. Conditions of this kind, even more than the maximum wage, tended to keep professional egotism in check.

The concessions that soccer had made to money were, effectively, a consequence of its grounding among the mass working class. As the audience was prepared to countenance professionalism, the game's administrators had to follow suit. Higher up the social scale it was much easier to pretend that the world of professionalism didn't exist.

Golf, for example, remained resolutely middle class throughout the inter-war period. There was a well-meaning attempt to found the democratic sounding 'Artisan Golfer Association' in 1921 – membership peaked at 15,000 – but with its pricey equipment, green fees and dress codes, an afternoon spent on one of the new suburban courses was well beyond most working-class budgets. In his review of *Cricket Country*, Orwell complains that 'the inherently snobbish game is golf, which causes whole stretches of countryside to be turned into carefully guarded class preserves'.

Even more than cricket, golf was responsible for some of the absurder manifestations of the amateur/professional divide. The great American player Walter Hagen, banned from the Deal club-house during the British Open on account of his professional status, took his revenge by hiring a chauffeur-driven Rolls-Royce and using it as a mobile changing room for the duration of the tournament. Several home-grown talents took fright at this hostility and departed for the American professional circuit. Some never came back. In much the same way as tennis, the increasingly professionalised upper echelon of the game would go on to create its own protocols, in almost complete detachment from the main body of the game. In this context the amateur Bobby Jones's victories in the British and US Opens in 1930 were wholly exceptional. Golf's future lay on the gleaming Florida fairways, not in P. G. Wodehouse's world of sedate Home Counties clubhouses, five-guinea subscriptions and middle-class chatter exchanged in the shadow of the Surrey pines.

VIII

'Play Up, Kings!'

The battle between professional and amateur was
not confined to the sports field, or even to the
administrative superstructure that kept the sports
field in order. Increasingly it spilled over into the
wider cultural environment, to the point where
much of the art of the period – low-level, perhaps,
but still capable of exerting a profound social
influence – adopted it as a subtext. The vast,
subterranean world of boys' school stories, bought
in their millions by teenagers throughout the inter-
war years, offers a devious example of how propaganda for the amateur code could be brought on to
the printed page and mixed with the broader social
atmosphere to create something that was practically
moral comment. However restricted its compass
and rudimentary its effects, *Strickland of the Sixth* is
much more than a novel about a group of boys at an
obscure public school who decide to enter a team for
the local challenge cup: its moral lessons weave
through the text like bindweed.

Something of this propagandist urge can be seen in the procedural deception that lies at the heart of many boys' school stories. Most public schools played rugby as their winter sport. Most readers of *Strickland of the Sixth*, *Shandy of the Shell* (1931) and *The Liveliest Term at Templeton* (1924), on the other hand, did not. They went to grammar schools or secondary moderns where the winter game was soccer. To accommodate this bias, the writers of school stories – often ex-schoolmasters – had to make their focus point a sport in which the real-life equivalents of their characters would not have taken much interest.

Neither, you imagine, would the real 'Strick' have found anything remotely authentic in the kind of novels written in celebration of his lifestyle and capacities. As a ten-year-old, one of my favourite books among the shelf of school stories handed down to me by my father (a rugger-hating boy from a council estate who won a scholarship to a minor public school) was Herbert Hayens' *Play Up, Kings!*. Three-quarters of a century on from the book's publication, Hayens – who wrote a series of *Play Up!* adventures throughout the 1920s – has vanished even from the reference books. I have no idea who he was, where he lived or what sales his work achieved. On the other hand, I have a pretty clear idea of the view he took of inter-war England, the legacy bequeathed to it by the Great War and the moral potential of sport in helping to right what had so clearly gone wrong; all this springs from the page like so many bookmarks.

Play Up, Kings! opens on a station platform with Will Kemp, a new boy in Kings House at Redfield School, being waved off by his brisk and martial-sounding papa. 'Now go in and win. Live clean, run straight and play the game,' Mr Kemp advises as the train steams in. 'And don't whine when you get knocked down. That's my sermon.' With this valediction ringing in his ears, safely installed in a railway carriage with various other Redfield alumni, Will is swiftly introduced to the principal villain of the piece, a florid nouveau riche named Marmaduke Howard, of whose family another boy remarks, 'Made a pot of money out of the war. Bought a big estate, and a fleet of yachts and automobiles. They are trying to turn Marmaduke into a gentleman.' Scented, bejewelled and expensively dressed, 'Marmy' is rapidly exposed as a howling snob ('There isn't much you can tell me about good society. We Howards belong there') and, as such, strongly opposed to the plan dreamed up by Clarice, the newly installed house captain, to regenerate a noble heritage by entering a team in the house football cup.

Despite the disapproval of Howard and his

satellites ('I don't hold with soccer. It is a vulgar game for the lower classes. I wonder the Doctor permits it to be played at Redfield') the plan is enthusiastically taken up and an XI assembled. 'A very fine show' someone comments (ironically) while watching them in training. 'That crowd ought to swamp the Corinthians.' Prior to the opening game against Pennycuiks, Clarice gives his team-mates a pep talk: 'Mark your man, don't get flustered, and, above all, don't lose your heads when you happen to make a mistake. Play till the whistle blows and play a clean game.' After a sticky opening session, Kings sail to victory and the opposing captain offers his salutations: 'Congrats, old man. It's been a hard tussle, and we're squarely beaten. Good luck to you for the next game.'

Against a back drop of ripping teas and swimming galas, Clarice's hotshots dispose of the School House in the final ('The fellows from the School were genuine sportsmen and they did not stint their praise'). Meanwhile, the novel's principal subplot boils comfortably away. Among Howard's hangers-on is a good-natured but opportunistic boy named Griffen ('one of the New Poor', offers Kemp's informant on the train). Taken to his patron's country estate, Griffen is shocked and at the same time fascinated by the pageant of counter-jumping opulence. 'The whole place showed a mixture of wealth, ill-taste and ignorance. The ghastly ornaments were new and crowded every available foot of space . . .' Hoping for some kind of job with the Howard entourage after he leaves school, Griffen decides to stick with his sponsor and, with the latter's sanction, agrees to join the house cricket team, from which a dislike of Clarice has previously kept him apart. Naturally Kemp, the player thereby excluded, 'bore no grudge against the Sixth Form boy, whose abilities he honestly admired.'

In the meantime, dense clouds of mystery obscure Howard's relationship with a studious and retiring boy named Cardew, over whom he enjoys some kind of sinister hold. After much high-handed treatment, Cardew's temper finally snaps: he hits Howard in the mouth and threatens to thrash him with a horsewhip. It is then revealed that old Mr Cardew, lately deceased, had been a partner in a firm taken over by a 'syndicate': Howard senior is the latter's leading light. According to his son, the books had been improperly kept and there was a suspicion of fraud. 'Of course he was innocent', Cardew junior explains, 'but somehow they had got him in their toils.' Happily a friend of the family has now unearthed enough evidence to suggest wrongdoing, and the son is to be amply compensated. The revelation is too much for the right-thinking Kings men, who contrive a special number of the unofficial school magazine demonstrating that Howard is not, as he has hinted, related to the ducal family of that name but the descendant of a Jewish old clothes salesman-cum-pawnbroker named Mosieski.

Thus framed, *Play Up, Kings!* reveals itself as an immensely pointed parable about the shifting social and economic alignments of Baldwin-era England, in which ill-gotten 'new money' is hard at work extinguishing the old-style gentlemanly virtues. Howard's fatal disability, it turns out, is that he will not 'play the game', here defined as joining in with house activities, not showing off, bragging about your wealth or lording it over more modestly accoutred contemporaries. For those unwise enough to break this essentially amateur code, any ammunition or means of exposure is legitimate.

There is a significant moment towards the end of the book when Hayens offers a justification for the Mosieski escapade: 'Had the victim been an ordinary decent fellow, Kings would have rallied round him . . . But Howard was a cad and a bully. He had swaggered so much about his family and his aristocratic name, had given himself such pretentious airs, that this anti-climax covered him with ridicule.' Kemp, the magazine's notional editor, concedes that he feels 'a bit of a cad' himself. On the other hand, 'the rotter's bound to go, and if this doesn't do the trick I'll try something else'. Happily, there is no need for further stratagems. Disgraced and humiliated, Howard leaves Redfield under the proverbial cloud.

Play Up, Kings! does at least have a vestigial grounding in a world full of ominous social realities and uncomfortable economic truths. The amateurism of the boys' school story of a generation before, that tide of late Victorian and Edwardian moral uplift brought out under the banner of the Religious Tract Society and the Sunday School Union, aspired to a purity of motive and behaviour that was almost abstract in its conception. The stories collected in Harold Avery's *The School's Honour* (1896) – another favourite of mine from pre-teendom – are practically chivalric in tone, awash with quaint little lectures on how to win (and lose) gracefully, suffer hard knocks with a manly smile and help lame dogs over stiles.

One of Avery's favourite tricks is to fast-forward his moral tableau through time and give it some epochal new dimension: the schoolyard tiff transferred to the battlefield, say, the sterling resolve shown in a sports fixture resurfacing in a matter of life and death. In 'A Lead Ball for a Leather One', Buller the scapegrace demon fast bowler, having dismissed two batsmen in successive balls, finds himself facing little Charlie Oakley, a negligible performer whose father happens to be watching from the boundary. Ignoring the chance of a hat-trick, Buller sends down a weak half-volley and gets clouted for three. The action then shifts to the scorching sands of El Teb, where a vigilant English officer with a solitary bullet left in his revolver takes careful aim at the dervish menacing one of his troopers and sends him sprawling into the dust. The thankful soldier turns out to be Buller. 'All right', Lieutenant Oakley assures him. 'You gave a ball for me once, and now I give one for you.'

An even more pointed lesson is on display in 'The Man Who Could Lose'. Here Bob Lowe, a proficient but slow-moving swimmer, is picked to represent the school against a rival institution whose pupils are known as the 'Blairites'. After a tight contest Bob loses by a whisker. Out in the street a confrontation between both sets of supporters is quickly defused when he steps across to congratulate his victorious opponent. Taxed with excessive civility, Bob angrily responds: 'Look here, I believe the next best thing to winning a thing is to lose it – that is, if you lose well – and I'm not quite sure if it doesn't sometimes show better pluck to take an honest licking and look cheerful, than it does to give it.' A brief coda takes us a decade or so forward to the packet boat *France* unexpectedly colliding with an unseen vessel some miles out into the Channel from Dartford harbour. The lifeboats are lowered and the evacuation begun, but the ship is over-loaded. In the end two passengers are left to contend for the final berth. One, who 'lounges carelessly against the bulwark', waves the other to safety. 'Your name – at least tell me your name', pleads the beneficiary. 'My name is Lowe', answers his saviour cheerfully. '"*Bon voyage*."'

Not all of Avery's work is so grandly symbolic. The value of the amateur code, to its early propagandists, was that it offered yardsticks for the most routine kinds of human behaviour. Opportunities for heroic self-sacrifice would necessarily be limited, but it was possible to display qualities of patient resignation, careless stoicism and proud cheek-turning in more ordinary domestic settings. 'Hard Knocks', one of Avery's best stories, has precisely this flavour – moral adjustments made in the context of a conventional upper-middle-class, late Victorian life. We first encounter teenager Tom Dawson crossly upbraiding his elder sister, who has accidentally smashed his model boat, and whose request to fetch a book from the town library he sulkily declines. Later, in the course of a hockey match Tom shows admirable pluck, gallantly saves a certain goal by taking the full force of a shot on his shins and ends up walking home with the captain, Winter, who pronounces a homily on the virtues of selflessness:

A man gets a good lot of hard knocks in life, many of them, like those in hockey, given him unintentionally by his own friends; they smart, and aren't very pleasant at the time, but if he'd only take them for what they are worth, rub it in, and whistle a tune, it would be much better than having a lot of rows and bad blood. But it's no good me preaching to you like this, for I know that you can take hard knocks all right, and you saved that goal like a fire-brick.

Avid to make amends for his earlier surliness, Tom dashes off to the library, reaches it a minute or two before the door shuts and collects his sister's book.

The average boys' school story may have been a rudimentary moral pantomime, full of keen young sportsmen itching to hand out socks on the jaw to their shifty-eyed opponents. On the other hand, moral pantomimes can enjoy a surprisingly long shelf life. As a ten-year-old, attending a school that bore practically no relation to Havenhall or Redfield, I was acutely susceptible to this kind of propaganda, yearned desperately to stand up to the school bully, believed implicitly in 'pluck', 'grit', 'spunk' and other Victorian abstracts and would happily have given a year of my life to captain the school rugby team or indeed achieve any kind of popularity among my class-mates, most of whom regarded me as a self-satisfied swot.

These attitudes, I now realise, dominated huge stretches of my adult thinking about sport and indeed a great deal else. As a connoisseur of international athletics I preferred Sebastian Coe to Steve Ovett on the grounds that the former was a clean-cut young Corinthian who spoke with an educated accent. It broke my heart once, watching a match between Norwich City and Tottenham, when Roy Race surrogate Gary Lineker, his back to the referee, beat the ball down with his hands as a preliminary to firing it past a suitably outraged Norwich goalkeeper. It was like being told that Bobby Moore had just been discovered snorting cocaine off a call-girl's navel or that Mike Brearley (a gentlemanly tactician to set against the beefy proletarian sloggers) had been arraigned before the MCC Committee for twisting someone's bail away with a length of fishing line.

'Serious' novelists, particularly those who had grown up in the north of England and observed professional sport at first hand, tended to be much less sympathetic towards the amateur ethic. *The Good Companions*, J. B. Priestley's bestseller from 1929, opens on a Saturday afternoon in the northern citadel of 'Bruddersford', as the vast working-class crowd streams home from a match between 'Bruddersford United' and Bolton Wanderers. Many of the spectators, Priestley suggests, should not be there at all. Here in Depression-era Britain, the shilling entrance fee would be better spent on life's necessities. In fact it would 'puzzle an economist to discover where all these shillings came from. But if he lived in Bruddersford, though he might still wonder where they came from, he would certainly understand why they were produced.' To Priestley, one of those archetypally bluff northerners careless of the civilities of the degenerate south, the professional game is a vital stimulus to individual and communal wellbeing, something that gives point to thousands of otherwise ground-down lives.

> To say that these men paid their shillings to watch twenty-two hirelings kick a ball is merely to say that a violin is wood and catgut, that Hamlet is so much paper and ink. For a shilling Bruddersford United A.F.C. offered you Conflict and Art; it turned you into a critic, happy in your judgments of fine points, ready in a second to estimate the worth of a well-judged pass, a run down the touch line, a lightning shot, a clearance hit by back or goalkeeper; it turned you into a partisan, holding your breath when the ball came sailing into your own goalmouth, enthusiastic when your forwards raced away towards the opposite goal, elated, downcast, bitter, triumphant by turns at the fortunes of your side, watching a ball shape Iliads and Odysseys for you; and what is more, it turned you into a member of a new community, all

brothers together for an hour and a half, for not only had you escaped from the clanking machinery of this lesser life, from work, wages, rent, doles, sick pay, insurance cards, nagging wives, ailing children, bad bosses, idle workmen, but you had escaped with most of your mates and your neighbours, with half the town, and there you were, cheering together, thumping one another on the shoulders, swapping judgments like lords of the earth, having pushed your way through a turnstile into another and altogether more spacious kind of life, hustling with Conflict and yet passionate and beautiful in its Art.

Orwell, to judge from his published writings, had no great opinion of Priestley, yet had he read this admittedly overstated and sentimentalised para-graph, he might have acknowledged that soccer, for the majority of its audience, was not simply a matter of young men kicking each other to an accom-paniment of lofted flags.

At the same time, Priestley's position, however sympathetic to the right of the working classes to enjoy themselves as they see fit, is never clear-cut. Only a page or two later, significantly enough, there intrudes that elegiac note so characteristic of any discussion of twentieth-century sport. On his way back from the game, Jess Ackroyd falls in with a friend who immediately begins to criticise a player for whom Bruddersford have laid out the unheard-of sum of £2000. 'If t'United had less brass to lake ['play'] wi', they'd lake better football', pronounces this horny-handed son of toil. 'Tha can remember when t'club had nivver set eyes on two thousand pounds, when t'job lot wor not worth two thousand pounds, pavilion an' all an' what sort i' football did they lake then? We know, don't we? They could gi' thee summat worth watching then.' Even here in 1929, with professional football only a few decades old and the average professional wage no more than a few pounds a week, it seemed already that there was something missing, some desideratum of spirit or endeavour gone calamitously astray.

Set Priestley down in a more bourgeois atmosphere, on the other hand, in an Earls Court maisonette, say, amid a chorus of public school voices and simpering women in evening dress, and he turns much less equivocal. There is an origin-defining page or two in *Angel Pavement* (1930) when the mysterious Mr Golspie, who has been shaking up the somewhat antiquated vehicle of the firm of Twigg and Dersingham, horrifies the dinner-party guests assembled by his business partner by maintaining that he prefers soccer to rugby. Major Trape, his fellow guest, takes instant umbrage. 'What, you a soccah man? Not this professional stuff? . . . I mean, you can't possibly – I mean, it's a dirty business, selling fellahs for money and so on, very unsporting.' Unimpressed by the major's insistence that sport and business are 'two different things', Mr Golspie offers a defence of the professional's craft:

> We can't all be rich amachures [*sic*]. Let the chaps have their six or seven pounds a week. They earn it. If one lot of chaps can earn their living by telling us to be good every Sunday – that is, if you go to listen to 'em; I don't – why shouldn't another lot be paid to knock a ball about every Saturday, without all this talk of dirty business? It beats me. Unless it's snobbery. Lot o' snobbery still about in this country. It jumps up all the time.

In the light of the novel's finale, in which Golspie is shown to have swindled gauche Mr Dersingham out of a small fortune and bankrupted his firm into the process, this exchange looks uncannily prophetic. Dersingham, with his Old Worrelian tie and his chatter about 'good sports' and 'playing the game', is an amateur adrift in a professional world – naïve, second-rate, manifestly not up to his opponents' fighting weight.

Three-quarters of a century later, this kind of ideological sparring has a rather ominous significance. To the more engagé social historian, England in the period 1918–39 is a nation fatally cast down by its reliance on an outdated, class-conscious and socially divisive amateur ethic. On one level – the narrow, sporting level – there is something in this argument. Certainly the inter-war era was a time when national sporting prestige sank uncomfortably low. Half a dozen major sporting associations – the AAA, the MCC, the LTA – were effectively controlled by propagandists for amateur-ism. The consequences were deeply unsatisfactory. In 1920 Britain won four Olympic gold medals in track and field athletics. In 1948 and 1952 she won none. Fred Perry's 1936 Wimbledon singles victory was the last by a Briton. Even soccer, the one sport in which professionalism had won a definitive victory, hardly flourished in international terms. English football's administrators, meanwhile, were an introverted breed, looked askance at international competition and pointedly declined to enter the first World Cup.

To the Oxford historian Ross McKibbin, all this is evidence of what was, in practical terms, a conspiracy designed to exclude ordinary people from sport. Bodies such as the MCC and the AAA 'provided a social exclusiveness and social inhibition whose legitimating ideology was the amateur code'. In pursuit of this goal, these institutions made it their business to promote 'social harmony' – that is, the interests of the middle class – by excluding those who 'didn't fit in'. On this scale of values clubbability was more important then winning and competitive play was largely discouraged in favour of social compatibility. On a higher level, moral sloganeering of the 'fair play' and 'good sport' variety eventually became a 'constitutional principle'.

Naturally certain incidental benefits arose from this discourse ('the comparative absence of political extremism in this period is partly a tribute to its ideological power', McKibbin concedes). But in the end, the lure of amateurism 'trapped the English within an essentially Edwardian political rhetoric which frustrated as much as it encouraged democracy'.

No doubt McKibbin is right to stress the innate middle-classness of much contemporary sport. The average out-of-town golf club was as impenetrable to most council estate dwellers as the House of Lords. George Bowling, the hero of Orwell's *Coming Up For Air* (1939), is keenly conscious of his interloper status among the tennis clubs of the inter-war suburbs: 'little wooden pavilions and high wire-netting enclosures where young chaps in rather badly cut white flannels prance up and down shouting "fifteen forty" and "Vantage all" in voices which are a tolerable imitation of the Upper Crust.' There were working-class amateur athletes who found the air of the northern professional circuit, which lingered on deep into the late twentieth century, much more to their taste. But in its purest form – the form preached by boys' school stories or by the original amateur teams – it was not in the least exclusive.

R. A. H. Goodyear, to particularise, was a One-Nation Conservative who clearly agonised over the divisions in English life, lost no opportunity to remind his readers of his characters' social and economic advantages and wrote another novel (*The White House Boys* [1921]) in which the heroes crown their sporting achievements by helping to rescue trapped miners from a roof-fall at the local pit. The Corinthians played matches against northern professional sides not to patronise them, but to export their own conception of how the game should be played to a wider audience. As for the idea that amateur sport was 'uncompetitive', it takes only a glance at the reporting of contemporary public school and club matches – see, for example, the epic house match final in Alec Waugh's *The Loom of Youth* (1917) – to demonstrate the extraordinary resonance of the passions aroused.

McKibbin does not quite come out and say that the advocates of 1930s-era appeasement, *The Times* leader writers, the All Souls caballers and the stuffed shirts on the Conservative front bench wore MCC ties as they dined together with von Ribbentrop, but the implication hangs in the air like wood smoke. In the higher scheme of things, Chamberlain might have been a self-satisfied ass who believed that Hitler was 'a great gentleman' even as the Nazis assembled on the Polish border, but set against some of the despots of the age, his own gentlemanliness, sense of duty, determination to do the right thing, can seem like a positive virtue. One can acknowledge that certain Englishmen were 'trapped within an essentially Edwardian rhetoric' while believing that its absence would have destroyed a part of England that, in an age of power politics and broken promises, it was vitally important to keep alive. A 'professional' politician, after all, would probably have left Poland to its fate.

IX

'I Paid for Everything'

Fanatic survivals are a feature of our national life. As a politics-obsessed schoolboy, I used to amuse myself by following the career of Mrs Annie Powell through successive volumes of *Whitaker's Almanac*. Mrs Powell, long since departed from the electoral scene, made it a point of principle in general elections of the Heath/Wilson era to stand for Rhondda in the Communist interest. The great days of South Wales communism were at this late date thirty or even forty years distant, but still Mrs Powell went on standing in election after election, racking up 1500 votes here and 2000 votes there and occasionally, in a good year, displacing the Conservative candidate as runner-up behind the rock-solid five-figure Labour majority. Why, I wondered, as government succeeded government and Communist representation in the House of Commons stuck at nought, did Mrs Powell bother?

Presumably her motive was that of the aristocratic die-hards who still, thirty years after his death, assemble in the Madrid *plazas* to celebrate Franco's birthday, or the handful of lunatics dispersed around early nineteenth-century European capitals who still hankered after the restoration of the Stuart monarchy: a settled habit, an unyieldable loyalty, a point that has to go on being made, however unpropitious the circumstances, until there comes a time when the unpropitious circumstances are themselves the point.

It would be surprising, given this fixation on lost causes and blighted hopes, if some of these survivals didn't come from the world of sport – not necessarily amateur sport, but that whole chaotic landscape of free-market, money-driven endeavour that the tidying up operations of the Victorian era could never quite extirpate from the national consciousness.

I remember thirty years ago, on a family holiday to the Lake District, being taken by my parents to an event that might have been called the Keswick Games. Here I settled myself down to watch – with a certain amount of teenage contempt – a band of rather dogged-looking characters in early middle age fling javelins and run handicap half-miles round a grass track whose white lines, it seemed to my exigent eye, had been none too clearly marked out. Local Rotarians? Inspired holidaymakers? No, these, it turned out, were professional athletes, the final beetle-browed descendants of Joe Darby and the northern road runners.

Like the last English wolf pack, hunkered down on Dartmoor at the dawning of the Stuart age, listening to the noise of civilisation moving ominously into earshot, they seemed faintly aware of the precariousness of their situation, conscious that the world had moved on, that the end of a line had been reached. 'Look at 'im', I remember some cheery Cumbrian bystander informing me, ''e's the English champion, 'e is.' I took a look at the burly unknown queuing up for the mile. No he wasn't. The English champion appeared on *Grandstand* competing in the AAA Championships, not on some lakeland meadow with a steeplechase in progress up the adjacent mountain paths and the hot breath of the Cumbrian wrestlers rasping in his ear along the trackside.

The amateur sportsman of the 1950s, back pages of *The Times* and the *Daily Telegraph* open by his breakfast plate, could have found plenty of evidence to suggest that the amateur ethic was still going strong. The four-minute-mile barrier had recently been broken on a cinder track outside Oxford by a young postgraduate student taking the afternoon off from his medical training. In soccer, the maximum wage hovered at £20 a week during the season and £17 in the summer – hardly a fortune in an era when a modestly successful insurance clerk might earn £500 a year. Billy Wright heard the news of his elevation to the England captaincy from the bus conductress whose vehicle conveyed him to the Molyneux. In cricket, too, the amateur gentleman, fresh from Fenners or The Parks, seemed to have been granted a new lease of life. England's 307-3, chalked up at Old Trafford on the first day of the Fourth Test against Australia in 1956, came courtesy of five amateur batsmen: Richardson, Cowdrey, Sheppard, May and Bailey.

Cricket, in fact, is the most shining example of amateurism's ability, in however bastardised a form, to maintain something of its original influence. Soft, out-of-season jobs abounded. R. E. S. Wyatt preserved his amateur status by working part-time for Sun Life of Canada. Such was the friendly interest displayed by the ball-bearing manufacturers British Timken in the post-war Northamptonshire side that at one point half the latter's 1st XI was eligible to play for the company team.

Even more important was the continuing symbolism of the amateur/professional divide. As late as the 1950s a message could be heard crackling from the Lord's tannoy to correct the score-sheet error that had let 'Titmus F. J.' (professional) into the proceedings masquerading as 'F. J. Titmus' (amateur). Meanwhile a few venerable and larger-than-life amateur county captains from the pre-war era continued to linger on the pavilion steps. Colin Cowdrey recalled an early fifties encounter with the legendary F. R. Brown of Northamptonshire – another ornament of the British Timken payroll – who greeted his opponent with the salutation 'Morning, young Cowdrey' and applauded memorable strokes with a cry of 'Shot!'.

Unhappily, this kind of thing was not indefinitely sustainable. E. W. Swanton might suggest in 1962 that 'English cricket has been at its best when there has been a reasonably even balance between those who have made the game their livelihood and those who have played it, with whatever degree of application and endeavour, basically for recreation and enjoyment', but by the time the words were written the balance had shifted irretrievably to the professional side. England's first professional captain, Len Hutton, had been installed a decade earlier. The percentage of amateurs in the first-class game was put at 25 per cent, while the efforts of some of the county administrators to cling to the tradition of amateur leadership occasionally descended into farce. The president and secretary of Surrey, for example, are once supposed to have been conferring on the desirability of appointing the well-known club cricketer A. C. L. Bennett to the captaincy when it was announced that 'Major

Bennett' was in the outer office enquiring about membership. He was invited in and offered the job on the spot, only for the interviewers later to discover that they had appointed a certain Nigel Bennett, whose experience was limited to running the Wimbledon 2nd XI. (In deutero-Bennett's defence, it should be said that he scored eight hundred runs during his first season in charge.)

The early 1960s marked the end of amateurism's direct influence not only in cricket but in British sport as a whole. The last Gentlemen versus Players fixture took place in 1962. Over on the soccer pitch, sustained lobbying by the Professional Footballers Association and the threat of strike action had seen the abolition of the maximum wage a year before: the archaic 'restrain and transfer' law, by which a player could be stopped from leaving a club if the directors disapproved of the move, followed in 1963.

Rather like sexual intercourse, it turns out, professionalism proper took root between the end of the *Chatterley* ban and the Beatles' first LP. In the wider national context, it is at the very least coincidental that the last 'amateur' British political leader (defined here as Etonian, aristocratic and sustained by exalted personal affiliations) should have led the Conservative Party to defeat against Harold Wilson in 1964. Edward Heath, who succeeded to the Tory leadership a year later, was by contrast a 'professional politician', a grammar school-educated meritocrat, appointed by democratic vote of the party MPs rather than the product of a backstairs intrigue. No doubt these distinctions can be overstated, but the spectacle of Sir Alec Douglas-Home, the 14th Earl, a fixture of the Eton XI in the early 1920s, going down at the polls to the Huddersfield Town-supporting West Yorkshireman had, as many commentators noted at the time, a resonance beyond politics.

There are other connections between Sir Alec's demise and the passing of the maximum wage. In both cases significant pressure was exerted by media land. There was, of course, nothing new in this. Professional sportsmen, footballers especially, had been celebrities for the past sixty or seventy years. Allowing for the inevitable differences in scale and courtesy, Herbert Sutcliffe, Fred Perry and the golfer Henry Cotton were the David Beckhams of their day. All this, though, was before television and the money that came with it. *Match of the Day* premiered in 1964. Half the nation watched the World Cup final in 1966. The momentum that built up behind the new breed of soccer stars – a George Best, a Charlie George – was beyond the ability of the old-style soccer manager to contain. Sir Matt Busby treated Best, whose career burned out in his mid-twenties, with an indulgence rarely extended to the Busby Babes of the decade before.

The most obvious point to make about this transformation – the gap between the nineteen-year-old Bobby Charlton's £20 a week and nineteen-year-old Wayne Rooney's £20,000 plus – is that there is no use whatever in complaining about it. The process was set in train around the time a century ago when Middlesbrough paid £1000 for the services of Alf Common and gathered pace from the moment a television camera was first introduced to a grandstand gantry. Either one has a free market in soccer, with Roman Abramovich and Malcolm Glazer circling the participants like so many sharks, or one does not, and the logical consequence is cloaca-tongued Wayne, simultaneously a footballing genius and the most unappetising teenager ever to have pulled on a Manchester United shirt.

Yet despite Master Rooney and his telephone-number salary, despite Mourinho's gamesmanship and the TV morons, amateurism's legacy to the modern game turns out to have been surprisingly durable. One can see it in the way that the game gets written about – no one, it might be said, is quite so fond of the adjective 'sporting' than a broad-sheet sports journalist – and in the kind of bedrock fair-mindedness with which (certain prominent exceptions notwithstanding) the average match gets played. After all, if professional football really was the kind of licensed swindle that Orwell and plenty of other subsequent anatomists imagined it to be, it would be played in an openly cynical spirit: a professional foul would be applauded merely because it could be shown to have prevented a goal, a defender sent off for crippling an opponent would be cheered all the way to the dressing room. That football isn't – quite – reduced to these depths is a tribute to the forces that brought the modern game into being and which, even now, are spiritually at large along its touchlines.

It can also be seen in the herculean fuss guaranteed to arise whenever anyone is found tampering with the game's heritage or seeking to exploit its traditions for commercial ends. Not long ago, for example, there was a tremendous row when the Corinthian Casuals – still going strong and currently ornamenting the Rymans League – discovered that their name was being used to market tickets at the new Wembley Stadium. Investigations revealed that a so-called 'Corinthian Club', a country club located somewhere in Stoke Poges and purporting to 'restore the Corinthian legacy', was offering ten-year membership packages at a cool £66,000 per head. The current Corinthian Casuals chairman, a retired Winchester College schoolmaster, suggested somewhat diffidently that the new organisation was 'not entitled to utilise our history without acknowledgement to our club'.

Curiously, there turned out to be a faint – a very faint – connection between the original Corinthians and the marketing men of the Stoke Poges country club. N. L. Jackson, who had founded the former in 1882, had been involved, twenty-five years later, in the creation of the latter. In fact the Stoke Poges Golf Club, as it then was, had once offered Corinthians FC a trophy for an annual competition. Thereafter the connection lapsed. The original Stoke Poges establishment, as the *Daily Telegraph* pointed out, had been sold in 1928.

In any other branch of modern commerce, one might have expected this lament from another world to be dismissed out of hand – 'heritage marketing' has produced far worse travesties than this – but no, all of a sudden the defenders of sporting tradition were thronging our debased modern landscape. The Ipswich chairman and FA Main Board member David Sheepshanks ('known to be a fervent supporter of what the Corinthian legacy means' – *Daily Telegraph*, again) was instantly brought out to remark that this needed investigating, and that he was sure 'nothing derogatory has been intended towards the eminent Corinthian Casuals FC'. A hundred and twenty-five years on, Jackson's star-crossed descendants – even now the only club in

England with its own coat of arms – are still capable of making their presence felt.

Meanwhile, what is the Corinthians' legacy to the massed and extravagantly remunerated hordes who actually play the game? The most satisfactory way of establishing what a professional footballer thinks of himself, perhaps, is to see what he puts, or has put for him, in his autobiography; a genre that, like the game itself, has undergone momentous trans-formation in the course of the past half-century.

The first sporting autobiography I ever read, plucked from my father's bookshelf thirty years ago, was Billy Wright's *Football Is My Passport* (1957). Pitched as a celebration of a career that had recently peaked with its 105th England cap and was about to founder on the shoals of management, this was a modest affair, in which hardly any information of a personal nature was allowed to get in the way of forensic accounts of such legendary encounters as the 0-1 defeat by the USA in 1950 or 1953's 3-6 Wembley drubbing by the Hungarians.

Not all old-style autobiographies were quite as innocuous as Wright's – Len Shackleton included a chapter headed 'What the average director knows about the game' and left the page blank – but their controlling patterns endured until deep into the 1980s. A few maverick exceptions notwithstanding, sporting chronicles – soccer chronicles especially –

habitually came to rest on a ledge only slightly above that occupied by a specimen issue of *Roy of the Rovers*. I once spent an instructive hour or so in the company of the man who ghost-wrote Bobby Moore's memoirs shortly after the World Cup: there was no trace of raucous Bobby, the trouser-dropping, table-bestriding party animal of late-night West End legend in their airbrushed pages. The punters wanted a stalwart Corinthian, defying the opposition e'en until death, and that, more or less, is what they got.

One shouldn't be unduly surprised by this. Most autobiography, after all, is an excuse to tell lies in public. It is the things that slip out by accident that give them interest. Whether the autobiographer is William Ambrose Wright, shaking his jauntily bequiffed head over Puskas and Hideguti, Roy Keane revenging himself on Alf-Inge Halaand, or Tony Cascarino with his worm's-eye view from the dressing-room floor, what emerges in the end is a version of how the subject sees himself, and – even more important – how he wants to be seen: that seductive 'personal myth', not in this case applied to the rackety cast of *A Dance to the Music of Time*, but to a collection of not terribly well educated young men paid large sums of money to play games.

What sort of personal myths are projected out of

the modern sports autobiography? Not long back I sat down and – not without some difficulty – worked my way through a trio of recent examples: Paul Gascoigne's *Gazza: My Story*, Alan Ball's *Playing Extra Time* and Alec Stewart's *Playing For Keeps*. One footballer from the age of scandal and excess, another from the more sedate late sixties golden age, when £250 a week was good money, and a second-generation Test cricketer known for his fanatical professionalism.

The first thing that strikes you about what, chronologically speaking, are three very different lives (Ball is sixty, Gascoigne in his late thirties, Stewart in his early forties) is the apparent similarity of the attitudes on display. Regular-guydom is embraced with the same enthusiasm as the phone calls from the England manager. 'We were all ordinary lads, as they were', Ball remarks of the England team's coach-bound progress through the thronged crowds of Wembley Way in 1966. Equally desirable is the lure of family ties and obligations. Stewart's debt to his father Mickey shines off every page. Gascoigne observes feelingly that one of the things that has given him greatest pleasure in life is being able to provide 'nice houses for everyone in my family'. Queerly, in both the Ball and Gascoigne books, a single phrase recurs in discussion of family affairs – 'I paid for everything' – not put there out of vainglory, you suspect, but to emphasise the nature of the duty done.

The other cardinal virtue, it turns out, is loyalty. Gascoigne never wanted to leave Spurs for Lazio in 1991, just as Ball never wanted to leave Everton for Arsenal two decades before: each had become a reluctant pawn in a corporate game played out high above their heads. Running close behind it is a genuine sense of pride – not merely in having represented club and country ('proud and happy to be part of the England set-up' – Ball) but in having clambered one's way up from the murkier depths of the social cosmos into positions of influence and power. Ball and Gascoigne wear their working-classness like rosettes. Even Alec Stewart, who attended a notably upmarket Surrey grammar school, can't resist a sniff or two about supercilious public school boys like Derek Pringle, who, the implication lurks, never had to try.

And yet the really curious thing about all three books is how little direct mention there is of money. One sometimes gets the impression from censorious sports columnists that scarcely a ball gets kicked or a bat picked up these days without a row of pound signs flashing before the sportsman's eye. Hanging in the ether above these accounts of Gazza's stolen fire-extinguishers and Ball's incendiary temper is the assumption that one plays a game, first and foremost, for its own sake, or for the abstract glory that participating in it brings. Gazza, typically, has no idea how much money he earned in the course of a lucrative career, nor where it went. Eight million? Nine million? Ask the accountants, with their £400 an hour fax bills.

There is a deeply revealing moment in *Playing Extra Time* (those book titles! How charmingly old-fashioned they are! How redolent of a world before Glazer, Abramovich and Co.!) when the twenty-year-old England midfielder comes back to the hotel room he shares with Nobby Stiles on the morning of the 1966 World Cup final with the £1000 each that is their sponsorship payment from the kind gentlemen at Adidas and simply cascades it over the bed like confetti. England's finest 'laughed like kids'. Oddly enough, in a landscape of seven-figure salaries and cut-throat competition, in which millionaire twenty-five-year-olds forbidden to talk to other clubs can claim that their human rights are being infringed, the Corinthian Spirit precariously endures. In its way, consequently, the average sporting autobiography is quite as 'romantic' a production as one of those shiny-jacketed Mills & Boon paperbacks with an evening-suited young exquisite on its cover, for it is practically the only place in which a professional sportsman can paint the pictures that most suit his conception of the life he leads. Perhaps, in the end, this is what 'amateurism' means a century and a quarter on from N. L. Jackson and his last-ditch attempt to stem the professional hordes: a kind of paradisal alternative moral world, where right conquers might and instinctive delicacy brushes away brute aggression, from which most of life, and nearly all modern sporting arrangements, are permanently debarred.

X

'I Could Do That'

Naturally, all of this has implications beyond the field of sport. If the Corinthian Spirit still survives, however precariously, around the long-off boundary and the Premiership physiotherapy suite, then its spectre still wanders disconsolately here and there through many of the corridors of modern professional life. That it can do this is a tribute to the startling resilience of Victorianism and Victorian attitudes a century and more after their official demise. For nothing, it might be said, has suffered more from contemporary notions of 'progress' than amateurism. The Western twentieth century may have been an era in which capital finally tugged free from the constraints of state economies, and in which some of the implications of the machine age became uncomfortably clear even to the people who benefit from it, but it was above all a time in which most of the formal processes of life were professionalised to an almost stultifying degree.

Nowhere is this transformation more evident,

perhaps, than in my own 'professional' calling. 'English Literature', my old High Tory history master, R. H. 'Tweedy' Harries, used to say, subtly propagandising his own subject to Oxbridge hopefuls, 'is something that an educated gentleman does in his spare time.' Born into the semi-professional middle-middle-classes, I knew exactly what he meant: 'books' were an amateur project open to anyone with a brain and a sensibility, not to be despised, but in no way as rigorous a course of study for impressionable young minds as, say, history or classics. And how – a question that hung over any agreeable-sounding vocation in early life – were you going to make a living out of it? I can remember once, just down from university in a year when graduate job prospects were at an all-time low, crowing to my maternal grandfather over a cheque for £75 lately received for some magazine article or other. My grandfather, whose forty-three years of paid employment had, like my father's, been spent working for the Norwich Union Insurance Society, was unimpressed. 'It would be nice,' he pronounced, 'if you could earn that every week.' Furious at the time, I now see his point entirely. Writing magazine articles, to someone who spent his days computing fire insurance premiums, was simply *not serious*.

Wildly reactionary when offered up to a greenery-yallery sixth-former in the late 1970s, Tweedy's remarks about what educated gentlemen did in their spare time had, a century before, been merely routine. No subject, it is fair to say, was quite so stoutly resisted by the late Victorian academic establishment as English Studies. An excuse for dilettante-ish chatter about Shelley, one grand Oxonian eminence warned when the idea of a Literature tripos was proposed at around the time of Mr Gladstone's last administration. When, in the early twentieth century, an Oxford degree course did falter into being, an alliance of etymologists and medievalists led by J. R. R. Tolkien and C. S. Lewis cheerfully conspired to ensure that its syllabus stopped in 1832 and was consequently devoid of anything much worth reading.

'Literature', as conceived of by pre-Leavis English departments, tended to be horribly abstruse, much exercised by Anglo-Saxon dipthongs or the identity of the Gawain poet, or genteely belletristic, in the manner of Lord David Cecil's lecture style as recast by his unwilling pupil Kingsley Amis ('Laze . . . laze and gentlemen, when we say a man looks like a poet . . . dough mean . . . looks like Chauthah . . . dough mean . . . looks like Dvyden &c'). Come Dr Leavis, on the other hand – and similar authentications were being practised by the so-called 'New Critics' in the States and by the early continental structuralists – literature suddenly acquired a whole new moral and theoretical context. It also, during the great wave of 1960s expansion in higher education, acquired a riot of professional protocols and the perquisites of a very respectable career path. David Lodge's campus novels *Changing Places* (1975) and *Small World* (1984), with their tribes of jet-setting, conference-attending academics, are a testimony to just how serious, how well-remunerated, above all how *professional* a business the academic teaching of literature had become by the age of Derrida, Juliet Kristeva and Stanley Fish.

And if the teaching of literature became steadily more codified and hieratic, so, by degrees – literally, by degrees – did the production of its raw material. Forty years ago the average middle-income novelist eked out the meagre proceeds of his books by giving talks on the radio or putting in three days a week in the copywriting department of an ad agency. These days, he or she can customarily be found administering Creative Writing courses at some of our newer universities. Not long ago, emboldened by a creative writing anthology from Birkbeck whose twenty-two contributors were all advertised as being hard at work on their first books, a *Times Literary Supplement* diarist added up the number of attendees on such courses and came up with the figure of 1200 aspiring novelists. Just as 'Liberty' in Macaulay's late-period political writings stops being a mountain nymph and turns, as one disillusioned Victorian critic put it, into the highly accomplished daughter of a nobleman living in Grosvenor Square, so literature has stopped being a matter of antic Shelleyan imaginings and turned into a branch of the civil service.

The resentments bred up in the average non-professional breast by the rise of the new 'professional hierarchies' are, of course, considerable. They are also, a glance at some of the 'professionals' sedulously at work in the upper reaches of British society insists, thoroughly understandable. Any reasonably educated and articulate person, you sometimes feel, could make a better House of Commons speech than the current Deputy Prime Minister, the Rt Hon. John Prescott MP: what prevents them is not lack of talent but sheer status. In sport 'professional' and 'meritocrat' are usually synonymous. Outside it, curiously enough, they can mean the exact opposite.

Inevitably, the gifted non-specialist observes all this in a spirit of profound disillusionment. One of the commonest notes struck in twentieth-century *belles-lettres*, in fact, is what might be called the 'I could do that' line, the laments of outsiders conscious of their own superiority but starkly aware that their talents are unsuitable to an increasingly specialist age. Here, for example, is the all-purpose literary man Beverley Nichols paying an inter-war-era visit to the symbolic heart of the body politic: 'I dined with Victor Cazalet at the House of Commons. After dinner I went up to the Strangers' Gallery. I felt how easy it would be to dominate the mediocrities there, but what would be the use? . . . If anybody spoke as badly as that at the Peckham debating club he would be howled down.'

A letter from about the same time from Richard Pares, an Oxford don of scintillating brilliance, to his fast friend A. L. Rowse, makes much the same point. Pares, who as a young man saw himself as a future Prime Minister, with Rowse as a Regius Professor advising him on clerical appointments, retained what Rowse's biographer Richard Ollard calls 'a dandiacal self-admiring conviction of his own superiority in other fields should he choose to exercise it'. Noting the early success achieved by various of his Oxford contemporaries, Pares complains: 'It amazes me to read of the boom of Christopher Hollis, Evelyn Waugh and Peter Quennell because I know I could do much better than they and I don't want the trouble of doing so.'

It is the authentic amateur note. Pares doesn't just know that he is (theoretically) up to jumping any hurdle set in his way, but he believes his superiority to be innate. The idea of the golden boy, a little of whose lustre is transferred to everything he touches, died very hard in English life and is even now not wholly extinct. Twentieth-century literature, at any rate, fairly groans beneath the weight of his exemplars. 'You're the flower of England's youth', someone informs Guy Crouchback, the gentlemanly army officer of Evelyn Waugh's *Sword of Honour* trilogy, 'and it just won't do.' Won't do, that is, in an age of rules, bureaucracy and zealous middle-class efficiency drives.

Curiously enough, the British Army of the post-war era was one of the last great battlegrounds in the fight between the amateur gentleman and the professional martinet, the decline of *laissez-faire* and the rise of zeal (a quality condemned even by Clausewitz). Anthony Powell's *Journals* contain a revealing account of a late eighties conversation between the diarist, himself an ex-army officer, and the historian John Keegan, then military corres-pondent of the *Daily Telegraph*. Powell asks 'about the fussiness one hears of in the army'. Keegan suggests that 'army professional Puritanism' began perhaps a decade before 'when those who had fought in the war came to the top'. Yet army professional Puritanism turns out to have deeper roots than this.

One of the funniest novels ever written about military life is Simon Raven's *The Sabre Squadron* (1966). A part-comic, part-sinister espionage caper from the early Cold War era involving a young mathematician who has stumbled on a revolutionary atomic theory, its ballast is provided by elements of the British Army of the Rhine – specifically a band of languid aristocrats known as 'Earl Hamilton's Light Dragoons' and a punctilious middle-class fusilier regiment. Though wondering how it is conceivable that a bicycle, let alone a 'sabre troop', can be entrusted to the care of the dandified dragoon subalterns, the mathematician, Daniel Mond, is captivated by their insouciant charm. The regiment, he swiftly discovers, gets by on a tradition of 'sodality', whereby most of the work is done by indulgent NCOs while the young lordlings swan about in brothels and lunch expensively in the locality's hotels on the proceeds of stolen army rations. Command, meanwhile, is exercised by a Major Giles Glastonbury, purportedly the Queen's cousin, who among other exploits fights a duel with a neo-Nazi who has insulted Daniel and is supposed during the war to have shot dead a sentry he discovered asleep.

There follows an outrageous comedy of military manners ('Do you mind?' a bridge-playing junior officer rebukes a brigadier who turns up with a party of official observers during a crucial exercise, 'there may be a slam on here.') that reaches a symbolic high-point when the dragoons are upbraided by the fusilier colonel for not setting up camp in the particular field specified by their orders. The dragoons defend themselves by drawing his attention to a memorial notice stating that several hundred political prisoners were shot and buried there in 1944. 'I always carry that notice around with us, sir,' explains Sergeant Major Bunce. 'It comes in handy if we don't fancy going where we're told.'

At the same time, the novel is a perfectly serious defence of 'amateur' values, based on a conviction that when the chips are down gentlemanly grit, and not being seen to try too hard, will see one through. At one point the terrified Daniel, holed up in the army camp with the secret services on his trail, asks his new friend Captain Fielding Gray why he should trust him. Gray offers to swear 'on his honour as an officer and a gentleman'. This is not Gray's idea of a joke, but the creed – even here in the world of Churchill and Attlee – by which he lives, practically the only romantic gesture allowed him in an environment stifled by dogged competence and professional nous.

The seductions of this kind of worldview are, of course, eternal. It was George Orwell, again, whose instinctual puritanism can sometimes seem a tiny bit excessive, who remarked that had he lived at the time of the English Civil War he would have been a

Cavalier as the Roundheads 'were such dreary people'. 'Professionalism' – by which I mean dogged resolve, niggling efficiency, mistrust of 'style' – came comparatively late to English life. In neglecting the tradition it supplanted, we neglect a vital part of the behavioural cocktail that makes us who we are and what we shall become.

Notes and Further Reading

(Place of publication is London unless otherwise indicated.)

I *1929* (pp. 5–12)

The account of the Norwich versus Corinthians third round FA Cup tie is taken from the *Eastern Daily Press*, 14 January 1929.

IV *Word-Hoard* (pp. 30–39)

For Martin Amis's account of the 1988 Republican convention ('Phantom of the Opera: The Republicans in 1988') see *Visiting Mrs Nabokov and Other Excursions* (1993), pp. 99–112.

Andrew Anthony's interview with Randy Spears appeared in the *Observer*, 1 August 2004.

V *Annals of the Corinthians* (pp. 40–60)

For Thackeray's attendance at the Boat Race, see

Gordon N. Ray, ed., *The Letters and Private Papers of William Makepeace Thackeray*, Volume I: *1817–1840* (Oxford, 1945), p. 48. For the statistics of public school land-lease and purchase in the nineteenth century and reproductions of the photographs of the Harrow cricket XI, see J. A. Mangan, *Athleticism in the Victorian and Edwardian Public School* (Cambridge, 1981), pp. 71, 166–7. Mangan is also the source of the quotations from Eustace Miles, Baden-Powell and Papillon.

For David Newsome on the rise of soccer as a working-class leisure activity, see *The Victorian World Picture* (1997), p. 222.

On the history of the Corinthians, see B. O. Corbett, *Annals of the Corinthian Football Clubs* (1906) and F. N. S. Creek, *A History of the Corinthian Football Club* (1933). There are also useful details in Josh Lacey, *God Is Brazilian: Charles Miller, The Man Who Brought Football to Brazil* (Stroud, Gloucestershire, 2005), ch. 5, and Alan Roper, *The Real Arsenal Story: In the Days of Gog* (Costessey, Norfolk, 2004).

VI '*True Cricketers*' (pp. 61–69)

For 'Shooting an Elephant', see Peter Davison, ed., *George Orwell: The Complete Works*, Volume X: *A Kind of Compulsion, 1903–1936* (1998), pp. 501–6.

in *The Complete Memoir, Volume III: A Patriot After All*, 1940–41, p. 183. Humphrey Dakin's memories of his brother-in-law can be found in Audrey Coppard and Bernard Crick, eds, *Orwell Remembered* (1984), pp. 127–9.

For the essay 'The Sporting Spirit', originally printed in the *Tribune*, 14 December 1945, and the correspondence it provoked, see *The Complete Works*, Volume XVII: *I Belong to the Left, 1945*, pp. 440–46. The review of Edmund Blunden's *Cricket Country*, which originally appeared in the *Manchester Evening News*, 20 April 1944, is included in *ibid.* Volume XVI: *I Have Tried to Tell the Truth*, pp. 160–63.

George Lyttelton's letter to Rupert Hart-Davis remembering the batting of R. H. S. Spooner can be found in *The Lyttelton–Hart-Davis Letters: Correspondence of George Lyttelton and Rupert Hart-Davis*, Volume Six, *1961–62* (1984), p. 115.

VII '*Mr Sheppard to You*' (pp. 70–82)

For Fred Perry's views on 'The Case for Professionalism', see *My Story* (1934), pp. 147–53.

The background to cricket in the inter-war era is discussed by Ross McKibbin, *Classes and Cultures: England 1918–1951* (Oxford, 1998), pp. 332–9.

The majority of the anecdotes that follow are taken from Michael Marshall, *Gentlemen and Players: Conversations with Cricketers* (1988).

VIII *'Play Up, Kings!'* (pp. 83–101)

For McKibbin on the socio-political implications of amateurism, see *Classes and Cultures*, pp. 377–85.

IX *'I Paid for Everything'* (pp. 102–117)

On the survival of cricketing amateurism in the post-war era, see Marshall, *Gentlemen and Players, passim*.

X *'I Could Do That'* (pp. 118–127)

The extract from Beverley Nichols' diaries is reproduced from Bryan Connon, *Beverley Nichols: A Life* (1991), p. 180. For the letter from Richard Pares to A. L. Rowse, see Richard Ollard, *A Man of Contradictions: A Life of A. L. Rowse* (1999), p. 71. Anthony Powell's conversation with John Keegan is recorded in his *Journals, 1987–1989* (1996), p. 165.